PRAISE FOR *BE BOLD AND WIN THE SALE*

Throughout the business world there is a severe shortage of good salespeople, partly because many who could succeed in sales don't have the confidence to take that crucial first step. Until this book there was little to help them with their fears. Jeff Shore shows you how to gain the essential confidence that is the first step to a great sales career.

—Neil Rackham, bestselling author of *SPIN Selling*

Be Bold and Win the Sale is not your typical sales book—not even close. Jeff Shore masterfully unlocks the secrets of busting through the sales plateaus that haunt so many sales professionals. Discomfort in the selling process is a topic that doesn't get much attention; Jeff Shore changes that.

—Jeb Blount, CEO of SalesGravy.com
and author of *People Buy You*

This book shows you much more than how to "be bold." It reveals a formula for structuring a sale that's pretty bulletproof. If Jeff Shore was trying to sell me something, I'd bet I'd have a tough time resisting.

—Marty Nemko, PhD, career coach and contributor to
USNews.com and AOL.com

Jeff Shore takes sales professionals where they don't often go—into a deep discovery of their own discomforts. Fortunately, he provides stellar advice and practical applications on how to handle and even leverage those discomforts. This is a book about exploding your success by busting through self-limiting beliefs. A great read!

—Brian Jones, VP, Divisional Builder Sales Manager,
Wells Fargo Home Mortgage

In *Be Bold and Win the Sale*, Jeff Shore shows you how to overcome the biggest objection of all—the one between your ears. Reading his book is like having a personal cheering section rooting for you and egging you on to act bold, go after the sale, take care of the customer, do a happy dance, and then repeat all of the above. Try it and prosper!

ncy Ancowitz, business communication coach
and author of *Self-Promotion for Introverts*®

You'll love the interviews with real experts in the field; you'll love the simplicity with which Jeff explains complex things like quieting discomfort and building confidence; but you'll put into action his really cool and usable tactics that will make a ginormous difference in how you win the game called sales.

—Scott Halford, author of *Be a Shortcut*

Wow! What an exciting and refreshing read in an ever-growing sea of mundane sales books. If you're a sales professional, this is a must. *Be Bold and Win the Sale* provides a step-by-step guide for getting out of your comfort zone and truly reaching your potential. This powerful, practical book is a confidence builder that will take your business to new heights.

—David Rosell, author of *Failure Is Not an Option*

It's simple and unavoidable—you cannot boost your sales until you dismantle your discomfort. Winners know this, and Jeff Shore offers winning advice for increasing those critical moments of boldness that define success.

—Ford Saeks, CEO of Prime Concepts

No one wants a hard-sell salesperson, yet salespeople who crumble in the face of discomfort will starve! Jeff Shore offers sound guidance on how to exercise boldness in the sales process with a customer-first approach. Any salesperson will benefit from his sage advice.

—Laura Stack, author of
What to Do When There's Too Much to Do
and *Execution IS the Strategy*

BE BOLD AND WIN THE SALE

BE BOLD AND WIN THE SALE

GET OUT OF YOUR COMFORT ZONE AND BOOST YOUR PERFORMANCE

JEFF SHORE

Mc Graw Hill Education

New York Chicago San Francisco Athens London Madrid
Mexico City Milan New Delhi Singapore Sydney Toronto

1 2 3 4 5 6 7 8 9 0   QFR/QFR   1 9 8 7 6 5 4 3

ISBN   978-0-07-182922-9
MHID 0-07-182922-9

e-ISBN   978-0-07-183050-8
e-MHID 0-07-183050-2

Library of Congress Cataloging-in-Publication Data
Shore, Jeff
  Be bold and win the sale : get out of your comfort zone and boost your performance / by Jeff Shore.
    pages cm
  ISBN-13: 978-0-07-182922-9 (alk. paper)
  ISBN-10: 0-07-182922-9 (alk. paper)
  1. Selling. I. Title.
  HF5438.25.S5625 2014
  658.85—dc23
                                                                2013032012

McGraw-Hill Education books are available at special quantity discounts to use as premiums and sales promotions or for use in corporate training programs. To contact a representative, please visit the Contact Us pages at www.mhprofessional.com.

To Carol Shore (1939-2013)
Thank you for your lifelong example of humble,
servant-oriented boldness

Contents

PART I

DEALING WITH DISCOMFORT

Foreword

As someone who has made it his life's work to encourage individuals to rise to their full potential, I am often forced to focus on what is "wrong" or in need of improvement. When I read *Be Bold and Win the Sale* by Jeff Shore, I found a refreshing surplus of "right"!

Be Bold and Win the Sale is an interactive resource for the person who is weary of the status quo. Jeff turns the daunting task of facing one's hang-ups and habits into an appealing, exciting, and profitable adventure.

When reading this book, one feels that Jeff is not so much interested in teaching sales as he is in connecting with each person he is "talking" with. Jeff and I are kindred spirits in that we both believe that everyone can make a positive difference in the world. Jeff dissects the realities of our restricting "comfort addictions" and leads his readers into a new way of thinking and working.

Be Bold and Win the Sale isn't a book for only sales professionals. Jeff's heart and enthusiasm for individuals and the sales process make this a "must-read" for *anyone* who wants to work and live better than he or she ever has before.

MARK SANBORN
President, Sanborn & Associates, Inc.
Bestselling author and acclaimed speaker
www.marksanborn.com

Acknowledgments

My name is in big letters on the cover of this book, but that is only because the designer could not possibly fit the names of all those who had a hand in bringing this project to its printed fruition. Writing a book is like building a skyscraper: one architect is credited with the work, but there are countless others who did so much of the heavy lifting.

Any work that is worth doing begins with inspiration. While all manner of people along the way can tweak and improve ideas and actual writing, it is a few inspiring individuals who are the catalyst for an author to sit down and write that first word. (And then to keep writing and writing and writing.) The legendary business thinker Mark Sanborn caught my vision first, affirming and then challenging some of the concepts, and even convincing me to scrap the original title. Cyndi Maxey (see her part of my story in Chapter 9) took a slow-moving idea and catapulted it into an action plan. But it was my career coach, Ruth Schwartz (highperformanceadvocates.com), who planted the seeds of belief in me years ago, and who has consistently seen more in me than I have been able to see in myself. Thanks, Ruth, for the constant kicking action in the direction of my backside!

Then there are those who gave of their time and expertise to add tremendous wisdom and insight to this book: Daniel Pink, Brian Tracy, Linda Richardson, Nancy Ancowitz, Larry Winget, and many others who have chipped in along the way. It has been both inspiring and humbling to work with some of my lifelong heroes.

I wanted to make sure that the message of this book hit home with sales professionals who are on the front lines every single day. A team of top-performing sales professionals volunteered their time to read the chapters as they were being written and provided invaluable feedback. Thanks to Dolly Majumdar, Cliff Stahl, Erika Diaz, Amy Wiley, David Huffaker, Marie Coleman, Tom Joyner, Marilyn Eliopulus, Danny Day, Ryan Taft, Karen Petri, Ashley Bryant, and Elisa Eesley.

Several people had a hand in the research, editing, and proofreading process. Tim Weeks provided stellar research from some top thinkers on the subject of boldness. Ali Westbrook served as a Jill-of-all-trades in coordinating details. Wade Mayhue brought finesse in the form of strategic direction, quote selection, exercise suggestions, and other compelling particulars along the way. Nancy Bach provided the left-brain detail work as she crossed every t and dotted every i, while I focused on bigger ideas. But it was June Steckler who performed the Herculean task of poring over every word and challenging yours truly to find the very best way to communicate to the reader. June proved to be the penultimate wordsmith, and you can thank her for the book's "readability."

I am deeply indebted to my agent, Sheree Bykofsky, not only for taking a chance on me, but for guiding me through every step of the process. I believe Sheree sets land speed records for her lightning-fast responses. She is the perfect blend of professional and personable. It was Sheree who suggested that we approach McGraw-Hill to publish this book, and for that suggestion, I am deeply grateful. My editor, Casey Ebro, has allowed me to write the book I wanted to write, and has provided appropriate guidance at each step of the way. And I am very grateful that she did not charge me per e-mail! My thanks also to the very talented team at McGraw-Hill.

I cannot begin to express my gratitude, appreciation, and deep love for my incredible team of coworkers at Shore Consulting. The phrase, "Stay down; Jeff is writing," was used quite frequently in these past many months, but in the end, this was a total team effort. Cassandra Grauer, Amy O'Connor, Kevin Shore, Charlotte Quider, Ryan Taft, Ali Westbrook, Wade Mayhue— thanks to all.

Our lives are much enriched by those people who come alongside us, offer an encouraging word, lift us up, keep us going, and mostly just commit to being there when we need them. Thank you to my friends who do this for me:

Eric Van Patten, Tim Weeks, and Paul Brown are my spiritual mentors and brothers in Christ; Carol Ruiz is the most interesting person in the world; and JoAnne Williams is my adopted big sister.

And to Karen, my brown-eyed girl. What an amazing journey it has been and continues to be. I am forever grateful that you know me well, and love me anyway. Dance with me!

Finally, I boldly proclaim that I am not my own. I am a child of God and dedicated to living the life he has in store for me. *Soli deo gloria*—to God alone be the glory.

JEFF SHORE

Definitions

Bold   Boldness is taking action to do the right thing, despite fear and discomfort. It isn't about being obnoxious, slick, or manipulative. To be bold is to initiate strong, positive action at a time when others would give in and take the easy path.

Win   Winning should be a group effort, a feeling of victory for everyone involved. All parties should come away believing that the mission was accomplished. Your customer's life is improved. Your company has gained a satisfied purchaser. You are successful, more confident, and living up to your potential. When anyone involved in the process feels like a loser, no one wins.

Sale   An effective sales process is about helping customers to improve their lives. Great salespeople first define what that life improvement looks like. Then they demonstrate how their solution best meets the customer's needs. Finally, they make it easy and enjoyable for the customer to purchase. A sale is a victory that all parties achieve simultaneously.

Introduction

*I do not try to dance better than anyone else.
I only try to dance better than myself.*

—Mikhail Baryshnikov

Potential is a beautiful and simultaneously scary beast. It can both motivate us and frustrate us. You know deep down that you can *do* better, *think* better, and *be* a better and stronger sales professional. And yet, as your conscience quietly but persistently nags you about the as-yet-unfulfilled possibilities for your career and your life, your mind constantly considers the coulds, shoulds, and somedays. Yes, you've got a thousand reasons why you *cannot* do this or you *should not* do that, but on a deeper level, those rationalizations always ring hollow. You are meant for more, and you know this in your soul.

The reality is that you have incredible potential and enormous capability, with the realistic power to accomplish amazing things and to conquer your most menacing demons. A voice from a far corner of your brain screams, "Break out! Be bold! Sell like a maniac! Live life, and live it to the full!" A countering voice says, "Later."

The origin of this dilemma is a common addiction. You/I/we are all addicted . . . to comfort. Like the proverbial frog in the pot of increasingly hot water, we have given in to a hideous and limiting habit of defaulting to things that are pain-free and familiar. In short, we live too much of our lives seeking comfort.

This tendency toward the comfortable becomes clear in our reactions to the common discomforts that we face each and every day. We see it in everything from how we approach (or avoid) difficult relationship conflicts to our choices in eating and exercise habits. The seemingly magnetic draw of comfort does not merely affect these choices; it is the primary driving force behind them. Our addiction to comfort is the root of such common maladies as procrastination, consumer debt, peer pressure, and most phobias. And without a doubt, this ever-present issue prevents us from becoming the high-flying sales professionals we are truly meant to be.

We see the manifestations of the comfort instinct in the stories that we tell ourselves—in our validations, justifications, and rationalizations for taking the easier route, even when we know it is not the best path. While these stories that we tell are familiar and comfortable, they are simultaneously counterproductive and crippling. The only "success" they provide us with is the means to stay exactly where we are, indefinitely. Ironically, the ultimate end product of a life spent succumbing to our addiction to comfort is an entirely *uncomfortable* existence.

But if there is a malady, there is also a remedy. The remedy for our addiction to comfort is found in one word: boldness. Your sales boldness is like a muscle group: when you exercise it, it gets stronger and stronger. Boldness is a skill more than a characteristic, and, like any skill, it can be honed and perfected. Boldness crushes our comfort tendencies, silencing the voices of our familiar stories. Boldness requires a clear and solid plan of attack, and the good news is, this plan of attack is readily available to all!

What are you truly capable of? What accomplishments lie within your grasp? What sales discomforts need to be beaten with a stick? What comfort stories do you need to set aside in order to unleash your potential and live your life to the fullest? Whether you are new to sales or an industry veteran, developing the boldness mindset will propel your career in a powerful way.

This book is about planning the attack on your addiction to comfort by maximizing the opportunities that are always in front of you. My goal is to give you renewed vitality and increased confidence in your ability to face *every* sales challenge and to produce amazing results. Just as the addiction to comfort is within you, so too are the tools that are necessary if you are to make clear, specific, and actionable decisions toward sales boldness.

Together, we will look into the allure of comfort and the inhibiting power of rationalizations. We will evaluate what happens at the exact moment of discomfort in the sales process and the corresponding decision that invariably occurs. I will show you a specific pattern for training your brain to prepare for these discomforts in advance, and assuring victory before your customer even comes through the door. Then we will dive into how your customer deals with discomfort, and, by way of application, I will show you a formula that describes the manner in which a customer makes a purchase decision.

In short, my goal is to help you develop the skill of boldness, knowing that boldness takes us to places that an addiction to comfort forbids us to travel. The challenge is yours if you are up to it, but it won't be easy. Get it right, and it will change your world and the world of those around you. Be bold . . . and we'll journey together to the height of your potential.

Be bold . . . and you will win the sale!

PART I

DEALING WITH DISCOMFORT

Discomfort is a normal—and consistent—occurrence for every sales professional. The question is whether you will accept discomfort as an inhibitor or as an accelerator.

Be prepared to approach the chapters that follow with a mindset of brutal honesty. Learn about your discomfort reactions and instincts. Identify the stories and rationalizations you commonly utilize. Come to grips with the important lessons you will learn about yourself and about your default tendencies. The remedies will be far more effective once the problem has been clearly identified.

You might find Part I of this book to be, well, uncomfortable. That's a good thing, because there is no change without discomfort. Welcome it. Run with it. Leverage it.

Let's get started!

1

"Well, This Is Awkward"
Understanding Sales Discomforts

Fortune favors the bold.

—Virgil

THE BIG IDEA
Boldness begins with discomfort.

I am a sales theorist, a student of the sales process. I hope you can willingly and boldly make the same claim. If this is our chosen profession, should we not seek to study diligently in "sales laboratories"? Of course we should!

I am not like most men I know. I actually love going to the mall. It's true, and I'll say it loud and proud: I love the mall! Why? Because I see it as a sales clinic, a shiny laboratory with constant tests, trials, experiments, and case studies, with the bonus of a hot dog on a stick included. There are lessons galore to be found in this big, air-conditioned, tasty lab, my friends—you just need to know where to look.

A TALE OF TWO KIOSKS

Recently, I was on a business trip in Southern California and I visited the Ontario Mills Mall, not because I needed anything or because I was dying to eat in a food court, but because I wanted to study energy patterns. I highly recommend this activity. Here's how it works: go to the mall with the intention of studying the personal energy of the salespeople you see. All you have to do is choose an inconspicuous place to stand, then simply observe the various sales professionals who are working independently but near one another in this "lab." Watch them closely and track patterns in their energy levels. Notice the intensity of their engagement. Are they really into their customers? Note their energy level when there are no customers around; is their presentation an act, or are they maintaining positivity all the time? Watch for what I call "facial posture," that lift of the face when someone has strong emotional energy. You can observe all these things without even having a conversation. You'll also find that when you identify a really positive salesperson, you'll just want to talk with her.

On this particular trip, I was studying a man who was working from a kiosk in the center of the mall, one of those sales islands amidst the steady stream of mall shoppers. His product was a therapeutic neck pillow. The idea is that you heat the pillow in the microwave, then place it around your neck, and by doing so, you receive some sort of healing power. (All right, true confession time: raise your hand if you own one. You know who you are!)

If you own one of these magic pillows, I can all but assure you that you did not purchase it from this particular individual. Here is what I observed: our would-be hero standing near his kiosk, product in hand, watching people stream by. Occasionally his body language would indicate that he was about to actually talk to someone, but at the last minute he would bail out. A couple of times you could see him forming words as a prospect approached, only to shrink back at the last second.

I watched this guy for five solid minutes, and he never actually talked to anyone. Why? What was his hang-up? Why couldn't he pull that conversational trigger? His job was straightforward: to talk to people about his product. But when the moment came, he just couldn't do it. Why?

Tell you what, let's get back to that guy in a minute.

I remember a trip to my local mall, the Roseville Galleria near Sacramento, California, several Christmases ago. My wife was busy shopping, but I was simply standing near the entrance to a department store, watching the polar opposite of our neck pillow sales guy. The man I was observing was selling nail- and skin-care products made with ingredients from the Dead Sea. Now, I know you know this kiosk, right? Malls across the country have enacted so-called leash laws that prevent these particular salespeople from moving more than five feet away from their booths. It appears that one too many shoppers has complained about the salespeople from these kiosks literally blocking their path in order to start a conversation.

So I was watching this salesman talk to one person after another, practically begging each of them to stop for a demonstration. In five minutes' time, I must have seen 25 people say no and walk on by. I also saw him successfully stop a young man in his early twenties who was sporting a tank top, a sideways baseball cap, and much-exposed boxers, as the crotch of his pants was down around his knees. Clearly, this guy was not the obvious target demographic for specialized hair- and skin-care products. But sure enough, saggy-pants dude walked away having purchased a full bag of nail-care products as a gift for his mother. Mall lab lesson observed: appearances did not dissuade our nail-care kiosk sales professional.

At this point, I approached my new hero and said, "I've been watching you for the last five minutes, and one person after another has said no and walked away. How many times do you hear 'no' in the course of a day?"

He responded in a thick accent, "Let thmee tell you. More zan one sousand times a day people say nuh to me. Chreestmastime: vedy busy. I count: a sousand times!"

I asked him, "How do you do it? How do you stay so upbeat and energetic when people say no that often?"

He paused for a moment, but then he really lit up. "Let thmee tell you. My prohduct . . . ees *so goood*! I feel thees. I feel eet in my heart; I feel eet in my seat!"

Now, I don't know exactly what that means, but it sounds really convincing! I mean, I feel stuff in my heart all the time, but I admit, I've never felt something so strongly as to feel it in my seat. The point is that his passion carried him through a whole lot of rejection.

I am insanely curious as to what separates these two salespeople. Are you?

COMMON DISCOMFORTS

There is a significant difference between the two salespeople I just described, and that difference provides dramatic evidence of perhaps the most important success characteristic imaginable.

We'll start with neck pillow guy. He represents a piece of all of us—maybe not all the time, but often enough. Neck pillow guy is a comfort junkie. He loves his security, and being outside his comfort zone scares the life out of him.

> *Discomfort is going to happen in life, and even more so in the life of a sales professional. How we respond is what makes the difference.*

Nail-care dude also faces discomfort—at least, I would assume he does. The difference is in how he responds to that feeling. His resolve is what overpowers his feelings, taking him to entirely new levels of success, levels that neck pillow guy can only dream about.

Discomfort is as normal as the sunrise. Discomfort is going to happen in life, and even more so in the life of a sales professional. How we *respond* is what makes the difference. The fact is that the sales process can be seen as a series of uncomfortable moments:

- The customer who won't engage during a sales presentation
- The prospect who won't answer the phone when you call repeatedly
- The prospect who is cold and seems bothered by your presentation
- The prospect who offers only vague answers to your questions
- The customer who leads off with a price/terms attack
- The customer who starts by addressing a quality concern, just to hammer your price

- The prospect who raises a tough product objection right out of the gate

- The point when you know that you need to ask a customer to buy, but it just doesn't "feel right"

Every single salesperson will face these moments as a routine part of her job. They are inevitable. Top performers find success not because they don't feel discomfort, but because they plan for it and are equipped to beat it.

THE TENDENCY TO "GIVE IN"

Neck pillow salesman has a problem, and it is a problem that we all face on some level. It is the common act of succumbing to our desire for comfort. It comes when we face an anxiety in our sales path (or in our job in general, or in our parenting, our exercise routine, or just about anything else), and it manifests itself in our response.

Researchers at the Behavioral Sciences Research Press in Dallas, Texas, study sales professionals from different industries around the globe and administer an assessment (called the SPQ*GOLD®) to measure various forms of Sales Call Reluctance. One such category of reluctance is called Yielder, and it measures the tendency to avoid the discomfort of bringing displeasure to others. For example, if a voice in my head is telling me that it's time to ask for the sale, but a countering voice warns against offending the prospect, the Yielder in me will back down and find a more comfortable path: "Here's my card; call me if you have any questions."

(If you have, at this point, become keenly aware of your own addiction to comfort, I don't want you thinking that I have cast you as a loser who ought to find another line of work. There is a relatively simple physiological foundation for this discussion, and we are simply clarifying the plan before we begin the attack on the comfort monster.)

Being faced with discomfort sets off a primitive mechanism in your brain that demands a response (it's a response of your choosing, but we'll get to that later on). To understand this process, simply go back to Psych 101 and recall the number one purpose of our brains. Do you remember what that is? Fundamentally, our brains exist to keep us alive. The brain works as a protective mechanism, constantly sensing threats and directing evasive action.

Consider the observation of John J. Ratey, MD, in his book *A User's Guide to the Brain*: "The physical and mental responses to fear were so important to the survival of primitive man that they remain very powerful and long-lasting. Unfortunately, this adaptive response is not always appropriate in today's world. Our civilization has evolved away from the need to overrespond, but we still do."

Discomforts, even sales discomforts, fall into this "response to fear" category. Our brains are wired to understand fear as a threat and act accordingly, with little effort on our part. While our higher reasoning skills allow us to discern the difference between the threat of a saber-toothed tiger attacking us and the comparatively mild discomfort of dealing with a nonresponsive customer, the primitive part of our brain registers both situations as threats, thus triggering what psychologists call the "flight instinct." This instinct is one of the voices that compel us to flee from a threat . . . any threat! No wonder the Dallas researchers came up with "Yielder."

ARE YOU AFFLICTED WITH THE COMFORT DISEASE? (UH . . . PROBABLY YEAH)

Giving in to our discomfort is a very common malady because discomfort is a reality that we all live with on a day-to-day basis. The question here is not whether we will face uncomfortable situations, but how we will respond in these situations.

> *The question here is not whether we will face uncomfortable situations, but how we will respond in these situations.*

This phenomenon affects all of us in different ways and to different degrees, and we all have different responses, but there is no one who is fully immune to it. If you want to assess your own sales anxiety issues, you can do so by mentally placing yourself in uncomfortable situations and considering your actions more than your attitude.

Imagine yourself in these scenarios:

- My customers won't engage in a meaningful dialogue, so I stop trying to bring them along relationally and hit them with a bunch of features instead. *It's easier that way.*

- A customer starts attacking my price. I take a combative stance in order to win. *It's easier* than trying to see his perspective. Or, I don't want to be the enemy, so I just nod my head and take it, because *that might be easier still.*

- A customer won't answer any questions, so I just keep quiet and let her shop in silence. *It's easier that way.*

- It's time to ask for the sale, but it doesn't feel right. I'll wait for the customer to ask me. *It's easier that way.*

- I need to make a prospecting call to drum up some new business. I think I'll update my Facebook page instead. *It's easier that way.*

Of course, we never actually get to the part that says, "It's easier that way"; that sentence remains unspoken. But the deep paradigm of yielding to discomfort cannot be denied; the paradigm says, "I prefer to do things the easiest way possible."

THE LAW OF LEAST EFFORT

This tendency toward cognitive ease is expressed by Nobel Prize winner Daniel Kahneman as the "law of least effort" in his book *Thinking: Fast and Slow.* "The law asserts that if there are several ways of achieving the same goal, people will eventually gravitate to the least demanding course of action."

The implication is not laziness, but rather self-preservation. Finding ourselves unsure of the depth of a given threat, we revert to the instinct of energy preservation. This subconscious tendency actually helps us to feel better about ourselves when we yield to discomfort. There is a built-in justification for doing so.

Of course, the penalty for taking the path of least resistance can be severe, coming in the form of limited potential and confining self-beliefs. Every time we give in to discomfort, we cement ourselves more fully into the familiar yet confining world of mediocrity. Just ask those around you who have taken bold but uncomfortable steps in their own lives. They will tell you that the so-called law of least effort is a sham, and that the richest treasures are not to be found on our existing mental maps.

DISCOMFORT CATEGORIES

If discomfort is a variable that is experienced differently by each individual, then it would be in our best interest to take an inventory of potentially uncomfortable sales situations. I will ask you to take a couple of moments now to think through the following list of sales discomforts and rate yourself (honestly!) in each category. As you do so, be aware of an interesting psychological peculiarity called the *superiority bias* (sometimes called *illusory superiority*). You need to understand that we have a very natural tendency to rate ourselves more highly than we ought to in any number of areas: cognitive reasoning, personality skills, talents and abilities, problem solving, even driving skills. This superiority bias suggests that we are not the best judges of ourselves. Therefore, it might be in your best interest to simply assume that you have a superiority bias and dial down your ratings a notch. (If you find yourself thinking that you are not self-biased . . . uh, case in point.)

Here are some common sales discomfort categories for you to consider:

- Prospecting
- Telephobia
- Dealing with people from other cultures
- Dealing with mean or rude people

- Dealing with people from varying socioeconomic backgrounds
- Dealing with objections
- Asking probing questions
- Price defense
- Demonstration skills
- Closing skills
- Follow-up calls

We will address these categories in greater detail later in the book, when we lay out action plans. For now, you can use this assessment for motivation and perspective, understanding that to the extent to which you remain unaware of your yielding tendencies, you can be certain to plateau at your current level of performance. Greatness will be beyond your grasp.

The good news is that the uncomfortable situations you face are identical to those that top performers face every day. Everyone has the same sales challenges, and everyone faces the same issues and discomforts. So, get it out of your head that top performers are never uncomfortable. That's ridiculous. It's just that top performers deal with their discomforts differently. Our natural reaction is to follow the more primitive directive from our brains, which is often simply, *run away!* Top performers have trained themselves to think from a higher brain center, a mental place that encourages them to embrace these discomforts as motivation. The concept is both powerful and liberating. Eventually, the activity that once created a disabling discomfort is performed without a second thought.

Where do you fit in this picture? Where do you sense that a sales discomfort grips you the most? For me, it was the phone call, especially the call to a lukewarm prospect. I have long-held telephobia issues (as clearly revealed in my SPQ*Gold® scores). I didn't like making calls, so I found every excuse I could not to make them. I told myself that I was doing the customer a favor by not disturbing him. I came up with other activities that would let me stay busy and put off calls a little longer.

What about you? Be honest. What sales fears do you most need to confront?

THE STARTING POINT: MAKING A DECISION TO TACKLE THE TOUGH STUFF

Thus far, I've approached this topic from a negative perspective, trying to get you to honestly assess your own comfort-chasing tendencies. By now you might be thinking, "Great . . . so I'm totally addicted to comfort and pretty lame about my desire to yield. Thanks for pointing that out, Jeff!"

> *Between stimulus and response there is a space.*
> *In that space is our power to choose our response.*
> *In our response lies our growth and our freedom.*
>
> —Victor E. Frankl

Stay with me on this, because the most important thing for you to understand is that capitulating to your discomfort is a choice. It may not be an overtly conscious choice in most cases, but it is still a choice. And if you can choose the comfortable path, you can also choose the bold (though admittedly more difficult) path. And that is where the treasures lie—that is where sales magic happens.

You have it within you to choose the harder, far better path, but you must begin with a plan to handle the tough stuff in your sales life. Don't start with your most crippling discomforts, but commit today to working in that direction. In this book, I'll help you identify your smaller discomforts, and we'll work up from there, but keep those "big boys" in mind as you go along. You'll see those challenges shrink as you formulate a plan and develop the habits necessary for confronting your fears.

PRACTICE ASSIGNMENT

Since we'll be starting small and working our way up, let's select a discomfort right now and find a quick victory. Think about some sales-related action that is not a particularly big deal, but that you've been putting off nonetheless. Pick something you can pound out in five minutes or less (two minutes is even better). Remember to check it off the list once you've completed the task.

- Make a phone call to a past customer.

- Organize a desk or a counter (if it doesn't require much time).

- Complete one "quick strike" item that's been on your to-do list for some time.

- Read a brief article.

- Learn one thing about your product that could help you answer questions.

- Practice curiosity skills by asking someone a few probing questions about his car, about what she had for lunch, or about his dog.

The idea here is to start small, so don't pick something that terrifies you.

Before you tackle this task, consider why it is still on your list. Why didn't you do it sooner? Was there a discomfort involved? This simple step will help you to identify your own behavioral tendencies.

Again, since we're in practice mode, begin by visualizing success. See yourself as handling this item easily. Look at the opportunity through a paradigm of victorious completion: "This is easy for me. It doesn't matter if it's a tiny bit uncomfortable. I am tackling this because I like to do the tough things that others shun. I embrace discomfort, and I *do ... not ... yield* !"

Now get it done—with a smile on your face! I'll wait right here.

(Hold music ...)

How'd it go? My guess is that it really wasn't that tough, but now it's off your list and you're feeling good about it. Let me ask you something: Did the paradigm adjustment affect your performance? Did the self-talk make it easier? I would presume that getting your mindset right made all the difference in the world, and that for some of you the task became downright pleasant! I'll address that phenomenon more extensively in the next chapter.

Note that I could have just said, "Go do something." But this was about your mindset, your motive, and your intentionality. You saw yourself as being confident and capable, and your purpose became clear; the action was almost an afterthought. Get the paradigm straight and everything else falls into place.

ENCOURAGEMENT

While we have started with a baby step, this is a potentially long journey for you. We live in a world that promises quick answers. I don't. Your comfort issues are longstanding and deeply rooted, and they won't go away overnight. But they will go away, one paradigm shift at a time. I promise you that this journey will be amazing, fun, and altogether life-changing.

Expect big things from yourself. Drive yourself to new levels. Commit now to overcoming your discomforts, and watch your sales career soar to top performer status!

Questions to Ponder

- What bothered you most about this chapter? What discomforts do you feel eating at you right this moment?

- Did you complete the practice exercise in this chapter? How did thinking about that task make you feel *before* you completed it? How did completing that task make you feel *afterward*? Was the task itself difficult? What can you learn from this experience that will enable you to choose boldness in the coming days?

- What mental approach will help you to attack your discomforts more aggressively and assertively? How did the self-talk help? Consider taking some time to write down some of that affirmative self-talk right now.

- Whom can you talk to about this? It could be beneficial to explain the yielding tendency to someone in your life that you trust and respect.

Expert Interview: Daniel Pink

Daniel Pink excels at turning tradition on its head. When I first read *Drive: The Surprising Truth About What Motivates Us*, I admit to having been downright frustrated by the fact that much of my thinking on the subject of motivation was flawed. With his latest book, *To Sell Is Human*, Pink single-handedly strapped sales tradition to a butcher block and eviscerated concepts that trainers have been teaching for years.

Daniel Pink (www.danpink.com) is, in a word, *bold*. Who better to discuss a book on the subject of sales boldness?

In your book *To Sell Is Human*, you basically eviscerate "old-school" sales and bring the exalted notion of the extravert salesperson down to earth. Still, there has to be room for boldness in there somewhere. How does one find that line between persuasion and pushiness?

Finding that sweet spot is definitely the key. New research from Adam Grant at the University of Pennsylvania explains why. In studying a sales force at a software company, Grant found that the most effective salespeople were neither strongly introverted nor extroverted. They were ambiverts—a little bit of both. They knew when to speak up but also when to shut up—when to be very bold and when to be less bold. Most of us are ambiverts, so instead of trying to be like the stereotypical glad-hander, you're better off being more like yourself.

Between them, your books *To Sell Is Human* and *Drive* shoot down just about every sales management tradition we've all ever known. If you imagine yourself in the role of a sales manager, what are you looking for in the ultimate salesperson?

It depends on the company and the industry, of course. But as a general rule, I'd look for people who are experts, particularly self-taught experts, in whatever they're selling. There's a huge premium now on expertise. I'd also find people who don't just have "good people skills" but are particularly adept at clueing into and understanding the perspectives and interests of others. I'd look for what I call "buoyancy," the ability to stay afloat in the ocean of rejection that is sales. And as discussed, I'd likely steer around both strong introverts and strong extroverts.

To Sell Is Human concludes with three suggestions for application: Pitch, Improvise, and Serve. Based on your observations and research, which of those three areas is most sorely lacking in today's sales world?

Serve. And by that I mean service in a deeper, more transcendent sense. About 40 years ago, a management writer named Robert Greenleaf came up with the notion of what he called "servant leadership." He flipped the traditional pyramid and put leaders at the bottom. The idea was to serve first and lead next, and by doing so, serving gave one the permission to lead. Something analogous to this theory is happening in the sales world today. There is a growing understanding that the very best salespeople serve first and sell next. In this sense, service means more than delivering a pizza in 30 minutes or less. It means improving someone's life and, by extension, improving the world. We can think of that as "servant selling," and it is the direction in which the world is slowly heading.

Getting Your Inner Boldness On

Sales Boldness in Action

We are what we repeatedly do.
Excellence, therefore, is not an act but a habit.

—ARISTOTLE

THE BIG IDEA
You are the sum total of your actions.

Larry Barker is one of my heroes. Don't rack your brain; you've never heard of him. Larry is not a research scientist or an athletic superstar or a dedicated missionary to a Third World country. Larry Barker is a bold salesperson—with a speech impediment.

Larry grew up in Charlotte, North Carolina, with a pronounced stutter. In fact, he does not recall a time in his life when he didn't struggle with stammering. Although he was constantly the target of taunts and jeers from schoolyard bullies, Larry was blessed with parents who saw far beyond the disorder. They saw a quiet boldness and encouraged their son to drink in life at every opportunity.

Now, many of you can probably look back at your junior high school days and recall the abject cruelty shown to those who didn't fit in. Personally, I was a choir guy, and that was all you needed to know about me if you happened to be a jock. The taunts were both inevitable and merciless. For some inexplicable reason, an appreciation for the classical works of Claudio Monteverdi did not rank as high on the Junior High School Coolness Scale as did the ability to plant a running back two feet into the turf on a football field. Just ask any of the popular girls. (Sigh.)

It is an unfortunate junior high school norm: if you are undersized or overweight, if you are from another country, if you are deemed effeminate or "butch," if you have a skin condition, or if you just plain walk a little differently, you are a target for ridicule. I made it through those days relatively unscathed. Some people never recover, especially if their "defect" is particularly noticeable—like Larry Barker's.

So what was Larry to do when he got to the seventh grade? The only logical endeavor he could think of was to join the drama club. I cannot explain this better than Larry does:

> I came to a crossroads early in life where I had to make a pivotal decision. I could be the quiet guy who kept to himself, scared to open his mouth because the words might not come out, or I could face my fears and take the hard road. My parents always encouraged me to take on more than I thought was possible, to overshoot my own capabilities. Reach for the stars. If you miss, you still get the moon.
>
> I made the decision that I would not let my impediment win. From that moment on, I began deliberately putting myself in positions, both at school and later at work, that forced me to face my discomforts head on.
>
> I figured that the best way to deal with the stammer was to increase the stress level. If I could get it right in the high-stress environment of the stage, wouldn't it be far easier just having a conversation with friends in the quad?

That, my friends, is what boldness looks like in action. There are so many lessons in that story that I hardly know where to begin. For the Larrys of the world, there is one consistent truth: you are the sum of your bold decisions. Bold decisions make for incredible opportunities. Today Larry is a top-performing sales professional, while the former high school football players are sitting around with beer bellies and living in the basements of their parents' homes. (At least, that's what I like to tell myself!)

WHAT MAKES A TOP PERFORMER EFFECTIVE?

Why do top sales performers do what they do? Why do they eagerly pursue business that others neglect? Why do they pour so much into their client relationships? Why do the best salespeople close more efficiently and more effectively? Why do they make more follow-up calls, and do so in a more disciplined fashion? Why do they move forward when others stop? There has to be an underlying purpose behind the actions of success.

I want to address this topic by encouraging you to look within yourself as I pose a thought-provoking question. We all know that having the right intention—the correct purpose—drives us toward success. We also know that proper technique is critical to accomplishing that purpose and intention. Here is the question: Which do you think is more important, intention or technique? I would make the case that there is no question about the answer. It is intention—a driving purpose, if you will—that makes for success in sales. If your intention is flawed, the best technique in the world will not save you.

> *If your intention is flawed, the best technique in the world will not save you.*

In order to get our heads around this concept, I'll share with you an exercise that I often use with sales teams. I take a group of sales professionals and divide them into two groups, then I send the teams to opposite sides of the room. I approach "Team 1" and say something like this:

> When we evaluate top professionals, we see similarities in their success patterns. Of course, all sales professionals have the intent to win, to get the sale, right? So what makes the difference? I would contend that the difference lies, very simply, in who performs at the highest level—that it is all about superior technique. It's like a downhill racer in the Olympics: all the competitors have the exact same intent, but who wins? The person who performs the best. You can have the intent to get the sale all you want, but at the end of the day, it's about the technique you use. Intent is vitally important; technique is more important. Do you agree?

Invariably, all the heads in the group nod yes. It makes so much sense, doesn't it?

Then I go to the other side of the room and address "Team 2."

> Let's be clear. We are in this training session today to work on your technique. And well we should; it is critical that your technique be as strong as possible. Here's the problem: I can have all the technique in the world, but if my intentions are wrong, my technique will follow suit. If, for example, my intention is merely to make a friend and I utilize perfect technique to follow that intention, do I make a sale? No! Our technique is driven by our intentions and our purpose. Technique is vitally important, but intention is more important. Agree?

What is the response? Of course, everyone in the group heartily agrees. After all, I am not just a sales trainer, but a salesperson as well!

With the trap set, I instruct the two teams to debate the issue. Team 1 will be arguing that intent is important, but technique is more important. Team 2 will argue that technique is important, but intent is more important. I try to bait the teams into making sure that the tone of the debate has a playful but pointed edge, and the salespeople always get into it.

The debates are always entertaining and intense. Since I have essentially set the teams up for a massive groupthink exercise, the arguments become more vehement as the debate goes on. In the end, I offer people the opportunity to switch teams, to join the team that lines up with their core beliefs on the subject. Few of them switch; such is the power of groupthink. But those who make the change always move to the "intent" side of the room.

I am an intent guy all the way, and while I try to keep an open mind about ideas and concepts in general, you will find me to be exceedingly dogmatic and adamantly unwavering in this position. I intend to get a sale, and so I do. I intend to eat a sandwich; my actions follow suit. I intend to sit around until noon in my boxers on my day off, watching *Jeopardy!* And . . . wait, TMI.

Show me someone with a flawed intent and I'll show you someone with an inappropriate technique. Show me a salesperson who is not crystal clear on the purpose, the vision, and the goal, and I'll show you a salesperson who falls short of his potential.

Here is an example of flawed intent leading to poor technique. Suppose I intend to ask for the sale, but I am leery about being perceived as "pushy." I propose instead to simply build the relationship so that I can ask for the sale at a later date. Meanwhile, a competitor employs a different strategy. She builds enough of a bond with the prospect during the visit to ask for a commitment in that initial conversation. In each case, it was the salesperson's intention that dictated the technique that was used. You can probably guess which salesperson had the greater chance of getting the sale.

Think of it this way: intention and purpose act as a road map to our accomplishments. The technique is the vehicle that gets us there.

WHAT DRIVES INTENT?

If you agree that our intention, our purpose, must be in place before we can utilize strong technique effectively, we are then left with an even bigger question. The intention has to be clear, but where did that intention come from? What prompted that purpose? I can intend to be a great salesperson all day long, but that intention has to be based on something bigger.

The fact is that the majority of underachieving salespeople get stuck right here. They do what they do because that is what they have been both told to do and trained to do. All too often, they fail to consider this motivation question on a deeper level.

Let me offer a simple but important premise: our purpose is both designed and defined by our paradigm, how we see ourselves, and how we see the world around us.

Our actions and behaviors (techniques) are always consistent with how we see ourselves (paradigm).

> *Your belief determines your action and your action determines your results, but first you have to believe.*
> —Mark Victor Hansen

Why, for example, are some salespeople far more effective at asking closing questions? The technique is critical, and the intention must be resolute, but the salesperson must first see himself as being effective in the ability to close. It is first and foremost about the paradigm, which drives the purpose, that leads us to the proper technique.

Here is the simple progression:

I am convinced that many salespeople struggle not because of flawed technique, but because of a flawed paradigm.

CONNECTING THE DOTS

In the Introduction and the first chapter of this book, I outlined a 10,000-foot flyover of the discomfort progression. Now I've introduced the idea that our actions, behaviors, and sales activities are derived from our purpose, and that our purpose stems from our paradigm. Let's put those concepts together.

> *The most important underlying premise behind dealing with sales discomfort is to understand that this is all about choices and not about circumstances.*

The most important underlying premise behind dealing with sales discomfort is to understand that this is all about choices and not about circumstances. You must believe that the choice to confront discomfort is yours and yours alone, regardless of your situation, your sales environment, market conditions, or any other outside factor. You must believe in your capability (paradigm), then make your decision (intention), and then systematically dismantle your discomforts (technique). In other words, I cannot promise you a bunch of quick sales tips and techniques that will transform you into a boldness champion overnight. The discomforts did not suddenly appear, and they will not go away quickly.

That said, I want to encourage you with this: over the past several years, I have systematically attacked the most significant discomforts in my own life, and I have achieved amazing results. I still have telephobia discomforts, but I have learned how to leverage them into creative phone energy. I do not have a passion for prospecting, but I have discovered how to channel the energy of discomfort into a clear focus on the prospecting portion of the sales process. (And my business has tripled over the past two years!) I struggle mightily with procrastination, but I have figured out how to trump that "not now" voice and turn it into a launching pad for getting things done. Moreover, I have applied the principles in this book in every area of my life: relationships, finances, goals, physical health, and more. I will show you how to do the same! In the process, you will learn how boldness is the single most distinguishing factor of sales success. In the pages that follow, I will direct you to one of the most important questions you can ask yourself: "How bold am I?" This question can lead you on a journey of both awareness and transformation . . . if you are bold enough to challenge yourself accordingly.

THE BOLDNESS PARADIGM

My daughter, Emily, has sales blood running through her veins. This was apparent from an early age, and as a sales trainer, I have always been thrilled to see her in action. Several years ago, my wife and I attended a fundraising dinner for her high school choir. (Yes, she too was a choir dweeb!) Emily was given the task of moving from table to table and selling a plate of brownies that she had made. She had informed me that her brownies were delicious, and that she intended to sell the plate of brownies for 20 dollars. I told her that she was crazy, that she would never sell the brownies for such a high price.

That was all the motivation she needed.

She quickly pointed to her "mark," a well-dressed gentleman who looked, shall we say, like he could easily part with $20. (Sales rule number 1: sell to people who can afford to buy!) The table was adjacent to ours, so I had the benefit of listening in on her conversation.

EMILY: "How delicious do these brownies look?"

MAN: "They really do look good."

EMILY: "I made them myself, this afternoon. I hope you don't mind, but I added dark chocolate chips into the batch. That makes them more chocolaty and gooier."

MAN: "You did a nice job."

EMILY: "You can take care of your whole table right here and they can all enjoy fresh-baked chocolate chip brownies. And you'll be supporting our choir trip. All for only $20!"

MAN: "That sounds a little steep for a plate of brownies, doesn't it?"

EMILY (with a ribbing smile): "Seriously? You can't afford 20 bucks? You'll be the hero of the entire table. And you'll be contributing to a good cause. For just 20 dollars. That's chump change to you!"

EMILY (to the rest of the table): "Who thinks he should just pony up the 20 bucks and stop complaining about it?"

And with that, the gentleman surrendered. Emily completed the transaction and then walked back past me. As she passed, she leaned down and said, "Do *not* underestimate your daughter!"

Was it Emily's technique that made her successful? To some extent, but her technique was based on something far more powerful: her paradigm. Emily believed in herself and in her mission. Her belief gave her the boldness she needed for this situation. It is that belief that sales professionals so often lack.

In a nutshell, previously unreachable success comes through applying boldness in moments of discomfort. The sales process can be seen as a series of uncomfortable moments; my aim is to provide you with ammunition to fight through that discomfort. This begins with developing a boldness paradigm. I can ask you to act boldly in the moment, but that action depends upon a foundational paradigm of boldness.

Think of the top-performing salespeople you have ever met. Are they successful because of their actions, because of their purpose, or because of their paradigm? All three, actually, but in a specific order. They do the things that top performers do (actions) because they want to be as successful as possible (purpose), because they see themselves as the best of the best (paradigm).

THE PARADIGM TEST

Now you have to ask some tough questions. I want to encourage you to take notes here, and to write down your responses to these questions. Doing so is the best way to get your head around this process. (No yielding on this!) I want to further encourage you to be brutally honest with yourself. There is no one to impress here—this is just for you.

- How do you see yourself in the hierarchy of sales professionals? At what level do you place yourself?

- How much do you believe in your own potential for success? Do you really believe you have it in you to be the best of the best?

- Are you stuck in the action dimension? Is your success based solely on activity, or is it more of an innate need to work and live according to your success paradigm?

- Is your self-talk largely limited to what you can't do well?

- Do you see yourself as the number one salesperson in your industry?

THE PROMISE: YOU'VE GOT IT IN YOU!

> *To accomplish great things, we must not only act, but also dream; not only plan, but also achieve.*
>
> —ANATOLE FRANCE

Here's the good news: you've already got what it takes, and that's a fact. Reaching the top in sales isn't about intelligence or education, or even about personality. These traits are important, but I'm going to assume that you are already adept in these areas; if you weren't, you wouldn't have been hired in the first place! But the answer isn't to "Just do it!," as the slogan says. That is a temporary fix at best. The answer is to change your paradigm, and in order to "do it" better, that paradigm must speak strongly of boldness.

I lived this paradigm shift firsthand when I wrote my first book, *Deal with It!* I have talked with hundreds of people over the years about their desire to write a book. It seems that almost everyone has at some point asked the question of himself: "Do I have a book in me?" Unfortunately, this question is typically easily trumped by negative paradigm questions: "Who would read it?" "Where would I find the time?" "How would I do that?" "What if people don't like it?" (We'll talk later about how to shoot down such questions!)

I outlined my first book in 2002; I wrote it in 2005. The story of the three-year gap illustrates my own addiction to comfort. In June of 2005, I attended a conference in Scottsdale, Arizona, entitled, "Managing Goal Achievement" (an excellent conference hosted by Integrity Solutions—highly recommended). As part of the workshop, we were each paired with a classmate and instructed to share a goal that had been on our list for some time, but on which, for whatever reason, we were making no progress.

I was paired with Gail Christy from San Antonio, Texas, with whom I shared a godsend of a conversation that dramatically altered my paradigm and my career. I told Gail that I had outlined a book called *Deal with It!* that was about handling tough sales situations. Here is that 2005 conversation as I recall it:

GAIL: "When did you outline the book?"

JEFF: "2002."

GAIL: "And you still haven't written the book? Why not?"

JEFF: "I'm busy. I have a training and speaking business to run."

GAIL: "Have you written the first chapter?"

JEFF: "No."

GAIL: "Wow. I'd say you are really, really busy if you can't even write one chapter in three years! Are you busier than Donald Trump? Because he puts out a book every year. And you can't write a single chapter in *three* years? Jeff, be honest . . . why haven't you written the book?"

JEFF: "Because it's hard. Have you ever tried? It's not easy."

GAIL: "Sorry, not my goal. But let me ask you: Do you write other stuff?"

JEFF: "Yes."

GAIL: "Like what?"

JEFF: "Curricula, articles, blogs . . ."

GAIL: "So . . . you can write. It's not too hard, or you couldn't even do those things. C'mon, Jeff—*why haven't you written the book?*"

(I have to tell you, Gail was metaphorically poking me in the chest—hard—and it hurt! But she was asking the question that needed to be asked.)

JEFF: "I guess . . . I guess I just don't see myself as an author."

Did you hear the paradigm commentary in that last statement? Remember the progression: paradigm → purpose → action.

As part of this workshop, we were given preprinted three-by-five cards that could be used after a goal-setting session as a way to encourage those we were coaching. On the card was printed in capital letters, "I BELIEVE IN YOU!" There was also note space where you could write some words of encouragement. Let me confess that I have a humongous cynical streak in me, so when I first saw these "I BELIEVE IN YOU!" cards, I could not roll my eyes back in my head far enough. "Oh great," I thought. "The happy talk approach." I vowed that there was no way I would ever use one of those stupid cards.

When I got back from lunch, I noticed that there was just such a card sitting on my chair. Gail had dutifully followed the instructions and left a note for me.

Let me pause here and see if you're tracking with me. What do you suppose that note said? Do you remember our lesson on paradigm, purpose, and actions? What did I really need to hear? Did I need to have Gail demand, "Write the book, you idiot!" No, action was not my problem. Did I need her to write, "You're going to sell a million copies"? No, purpose was not my problem. I had a paradigm problem, and that is what Gail addressed by writing four words in huge letters across the top of the card.

And here it is, the very "I BELIEVE IN YOU!" card that Gail wrote to me in 2005. I have kept it all these years.

Notice those four words: "I AM AN AUTHOR." Those are paradigm-changing words.

When I saw that note card, my first impression was, "Oh, isn't that sweet of her." Really, it was a kind gesture on Gail's part, but that was about it. When I got back from the conference, I didn't know what to do with the card, but I didn't want to throw it away, so I placed it on the shelf next to my desk, a pleasant reminder of a great conference.

Two weeks later, something strange happened. I woke up at 6:00 on a Saturday morning. (Trust me—that qualifies as strange for me!) I was wide awake, so I walked over to my computer and started to write. The next morning, it happened again. Two weeks later, I had completed the entire first draft of *Deal with It!*, a book that is now in its second edition and seventh printing. I've sold thousands and thousands of copies over the years, and I can honestly say that it has been one of the most successful and rewarding endeavors of my professional career. And it all goes back to one conversation, in which Gail Christy challenged my boldness paradigm.

GETTING YOUR BOLD ON

My friends, may I humbly but boldly suggest that you need to go on a journey to get your head right. The most important sales presentation you will ever give will be the one that convinces you to believe in yourself.

> *The most important sales presentation you will ever give will be the one that convinces you to believe in yourself.*

While it is critical that we get the success paradigm part right, this book is about one particular aspect of the paradigm: the boldness element. Soon we will dive into the part of your paradigm that holds you back. We'll identify a critical stumbling block that afflicts every sales presentation. We'll look at one particular paradigm change that will make all the difference in the world. By the time we're done, you'll have not just a whole new way of seeing your world (paradigm), but a whole new purpose and, yes, a whole new technique as well.

If you scan the table of contents, you'll see that this is not a sales technique book, but rather a sales mindset book. Get the mindset right, and the technique will follow—I promise you that.

And let me share one mindset that will help you to understand my intention. Boldness is not about being slick, manipulative, or obnoxious. I'll address this more in Chapter 6, but for now I would like you to be comfortable with the idea of "humble boldness," a mental paradigm that suggests that boldness is something to be exercised in the best interest of others. Humility and boldness are two traits that work together quite nicely.

BRUTAL HONESTY

This book is also about exorcising the self-limiting demons that haunt your sales career. As I did in overcoming my fear of writing a book, you're going to need to unlearn deep-rooted thought patterns and come to grips with stories (lies!) that you've been telling yourself. Fair warning: there are specific and often uncomfortable exercises in the pages that follow. Mostly, you'll need to be deeply introspective and brutally honest. This is not a book that you want to get something out of; it is a book that is designed to get something out of you.

As we launch into the how-to portion of the book, I encourage you to read actively, with pen and journal in hand. Highlight and dog-ear it like crazy. Make this book an active journey rather than just a "good read." Share your insights and discoveries with others, and, if you're really bold, apply the principles you find here to other areas of your life.

Let me repeat: you've already got it in you. You have within you the seeds of greatness. Now you need to plant those seeds and let them flourish.

Buckle up and get ready for the ride of your sales life!

Questions to Ponder

What has made you effective up to this point in your career? What are the paradigms of success that you have leveraged for great achievement thus far?

What self-talk messages need to be programmed (or reprogrammed)? What is stopping you from doing that right away?

What big goal could you begin to pursue simply by getting your paradigm right?

Expert Interview: Tom Daves

With more than 80,000 agents, Keller Williams is the largest real estate firm in the United States (by agent count). The number one agent at Keller Williams for three of the last five years has been Tom Daves, a 35-year-plus sales veteran who has seen and done it all. Whether it is residential sales, commercial sales, bank-owned property sales, flipping, or management, Tom Daves is a master.

Real estate is an extremely competitive business with an alarmingly high agent turnover rate. Rising to the top calls for dogged determination and a willingness to work through massive discomfort. Tom Daves knows that better than anyone.

You have achieved extraordinary success in a business that is highly cyclical, especially in the California marketplace where you work. How do you stay on top?

One of my favorite quotes is from Wayne Gretzky, who said, "Skate to where the puck is going to be." I always want to be in front of the market and anticipating where it is going. I am primarily a listing agent, but I switched to working more with buyers in the bank-owned days. Markets change. Business changes. When you get stuck doing what you've always done, you are vulnerable.

Was there ever a time when you were slow to react to changes in the market?

In the early 2000s, I worked a great deal with investors, and that led me into the flipping business. I would buy, renovate, and flip homes, and I experienced great success. I bought and sold 150 homes over a two-year period of time, and

I made a ton of money. But then the market turned, and I was slow to embrace that turn. I was comfortable with my success, and that comfort made me slow to react.

Yet you describe yourself as "skating to where the puck is going to be" and even pride yourself on it. What happened?

I think it's what your book is all about. We get sucked into a comfortable rut. If we are good at what we do and are comfortable with our daily activities, that causes us to stay where we are. At first we're in a groove, but before we know it, we're in a rut, and if we don't change, we'll end up in a grave!

Prospecting for new business is one of the great discomforts for so many salespeople. How do you approach that?

I'll be honest—it was really hard early in my career. I was really uncomfortable, but I was also really determined. I started out in real estate doing anything and everything: holding open houses, knocking on doors, cold calling, etc. I found that if I was going to be successful over the long term, I needed to focus on both what I was good at and what I enjoyed doing. For me, that meant specializing in working with sellers, becoming a listing agent. If you focus on what you're good at, you maximize your own capabilities and opportunities.

How do you deal with discomfort?

I go back to the basics. I go back to those early days in my career when I was most uncomfortable, but I just did it anyway. When you do something over and over, it becomes more and more comfortable. Then, after a while, you don't even think about it.

These days, you're flying to New York and talking to high-powered Wall Street types about investing millions. Is that intimidating? Is it uncomfortable?

This business is really all about relationships, even for the Wall Street types. I'm really good at what I do, and I really enjoy it. Is it intimidating? Absolutely! I'm a nervous wreck the entire flight. But then I remember that these are real people, and they have real lives and real objectives. I use the power of relationship and go from there. Success is a tremendous rush. The plane ride home is a thrill of victory.

Is it a stretch to say that you actually enjoy discomfort?

I think it's more accurate to say that I get a rush when I do uncomfortable things. The success makes me think bigger, and then I want to do more. Overcoming discomfort makes me stronger for the next opportunity.

What advice do you have for someone who is brand new to the sales business?

First, connect with an organization that supports your values. Don't even deal with the discomfort of being with a firm that makes you uncomfortable because your ethical standard is different than theirs. You can't be successful in that environment. Second, discover what makes you great, and do the uncomfortable things within that niche. It's a whole lot more enjoyable to do the uncomfortable things that are consistent with your version of success.

That Nagging Squirminess
Discomforts and Decisions

"Life is pain, Highness.
Anyone who says differently is selling something."

—WESTLEY IN *THE PRINCESS BRIDE*

THE BIG IDEA
A Moment of Discomfort always leads to
a Moment of Decision

"**L**ife is hard."

Those are the opening words of M. Scott Peck's *The Road Less Traveled*, the landmark work on living a fulfilled life. Peck goes on to suggest, "We must attest to the fact that life was never meant to be easy, and that it is nothing but a battlefield of problems. We can either moan about them or solve them. It is here that the vital role of discipline assumes significance."

There is a certain normalcy in the difficulty of life, just as, I believe, there is a normalcy in the discomfort of sales. We need not apologize for this uneasiness, nor should we experience even the slightest degree of guilt or shame. It should come as no surprise to us that sales discomfort is an entirely natural phenomenon.

It is in the reaction to discomfort that we find the separation between top performers and everyone else. You might have heard the adage, "Pain is inevitable; misery is a choice." This same idea applies to discomfort. Sales discomfort is normal; how you handle it is up to you.

In this chapter, I hope to challenge you on an even deeper level. I have spent a great deal of time thinking about and researching a straightforward, yet profound question: is discomfort a good thing or a bad thing? The answer depends on your perspective.

My sofa is comfortable; my elliptical machine is not. Cheeseburgers are comfortable; broccoli is not. That is one perspective on discomfort versus comfort. Here is another.

Being overweight and out of shape is a worse reality than the discomfort of eating right and exercising. I will sacrifice the cheap, temporary comfort of poor eating and lounging on the couch in order to find success, satisfaction, and renewed energy through embracing the discomfort of eating right and exercising.

It's all about your perspective.

LIFE DISCOMFORTS

I would stop short of describing myself as a history buff (perhaps the word *enthusiast* would be more fitting), but I confess to having a keen interest in early U.S. history. The battle for independence and the formation of the country make for fascinating study. If you've never read David McCullough's Pulitzer Prize–winning biography of John Adams, you are seriously missing out. This is a truly transformational book, and it will forever reshape your understanding of the American Revolution.

The book describes all kinds of things that I find admirable about our country's founding fathers, but the thing that is most striking to me is the normalcy of discomfort in their day-to-day living. Voyages to Europe to gain international support took weeks and endangered the lives of all on board. The British military was well armed and well trained. Loyalists made every conversation suspect. Nothing that met regular food, shelter, and health needs was convenient or easy to come by. And once the Declaration of Independence was adopted, the very real discomfort of war began.

For the founders of our nation, discomfort was a fact of life. Moreover, it was a necessary precursor for change. To put it another way, the discomfort brought about by the revolution was one indication that it was a cause worth fighting for.

Let me offer another example. I would also stop short of saying that I am a fitness buff (perhaps the phrase *not a total slug* would be more fitting), but I do appreciate a good hard workout. To me, the best workouts are the ones where I feel like I leave everything "on the table" and walk away feeling totally spent and utterly satisfied.

> *Strength does not come from winning. Your struggles develop your strengths. When you go through hardships and decide not to surrender, that is strength.*
>
> —Arnold Schwarzenegger

Perhaps you are old enough to remember when Arnold Schwarzenegger was known not for action movies or for politics, but for bodybuilding. He promoted the idea that, "Strength does not come from winning. Your struggles develop your strengths. When you go through hardships and decide not to surrender, that is strength." To a bodybuilder, discomfort is as natural as breathing. It is something to be embraced, not something to be avoided. It is only through discomfort that progress is truly made.

In addition to my nonexpert status in history and fitness, to say that I "play the piano" would also be a stretch. If you are sensitive to sour notes, you should stay away; my piano playing has been described as "lemonade-like." Because I understand the difficulty of the instrument, I have great respect for those who have logged countless hours in an area of discomfort called practice. Scales, etudes, chord progressions, circle of fifths . . . it's not for me. I just want to play. But without the discomfort of diligent practice, I can never expect to be truly great.

The absolute necessity of choosing discomfort in order to excel is true in music, athletics, theater, surgery . . . and sales. Practice is a discomfort that many professionals wish to ignore. But when you look at the best of the best in every category, you will find that a dedication to practice is what sets the top performers apart. It is not a matter of whether practice is uncomfortable. Skipping practice is simply not a consideration.

> *The destination called mastery lies on a road called repetition.*

THE DISCOMFORT BENEFIT

The necessity of practice (despite the discomfort) proves an important premise about sales and about life: growth begins at the point of discomfort. If you miss that, you have missed one of the most important points in this book. Growth *begins* with discomfort.

To put it another way, there is no growth in the absence of discomfort. Now, you can choose to interpret that in whatever way you wish. For some, the response will be, "Shoot. I was hoping to find an easy way. Now I'll never really grow." I believe that this response is nothing but a manifestation of a finely tuned addiction to comfort. It is more comfortable to assume that you don't have it in you than to accept the fact that you do! I hope *your* response is more like this: "If that's the case, bring it on!" Even if you don't fully believe that you are ready to bring discomfort on yourself, let your desire to excel overpower any default tendency you have to assume that you can't handle discomfort. Contrary to what Jack Nicholson said, you *can* handle the truth! And the truth is, you can handle the discomfort of growth. You are made for it.

EMBRACING DISCOMFORT

Clearly, this is not a "how-to" book on eliminating sales discomfort. That would amount to a fool's errand. In fact, this book isn't even about overcoming discomfort. That would imply that discomfort is some kind of evil enemy that is crouching around the corner, waiting to pounce. This book is about embracing discomfort. I would love nothing more than for sales professionals to recognize their common discomforts and react with spirited fist pumps! It is no longer about letting your conscience alone be your guide, but about letting your discomfort lead you to new levels of performance.

> *The obstacle is the path.*
>
> —ZEN PROVERB

I'm not much of a Zen guy, but I love this saying: "The obstacle is the path." Or to put that another way, "The obstacle *is* the path." Many people believe that obstacles prevent us from moving down the path of success, or that the path is somehow less desirable because of the obstacles. But to see that the obstacle is itself one's path—that's a game changer.

Think about your sales goals for a moment. Are they aggressive? Scary even? When you look at the number of clients you will need to talk to and the number of calls you will need to make to achieve your goals, do they frighten you? They should! If your goals are not intimidating and uncomfortable, you need to increase the target. (Or at least stop calling them "goals." Call them what they are: "sames." But don't. You are better than that!)

Think of it this way: if the obstacles on the way to a goal are relatively minor, it isn't much of a goal! The presence of obstacles is validation that you are, in fact, heading in the right direction.

I want to give you permission to be uncomfortable. Feel free to be as uneasy as you want to be . . . for now. Be the voice that tells your own brain that you will turn that discomfort into a stepping-stone (or even a launchpad!) for your future success.

IDENTIFYING PRIMARY SALES DISCOMFORTS

Discomforts come in all shapes and sizes. Hopefully, by this point you have already come to recognize some of the areas of discomfort in your sales life. To help you gain greater clarity in that discovery process, I will ask you to spend some time filling out the chart below. Simply indicate your level of discomfort—high, medium, or low—in each sales situation. Depending on your sales environment, not all discomfort categories will apply. This list is not exhaustive, so feel free to add to it.

Take some time and really think these things through. Be honest, and if you're not sure how to answer, you should just assume that you have some discomfort in that area!

Sales Discomforts	Low	Medium	High
Making an initial prospecting call	○	○	○
Making a follow-up prospecting call	○	○	○
Dealing with the "gatekeeper"	○	○	○
Closing on an initial appointment	○	○	○
Shaking hands during the greeting	○	○	○
Rapport-building conversations	○	○	○
Communicating effectively to more than one decision maker	○	○	○
Dealing with people who are initially cold, curt, or impatient	○	○	○
Asking about the current pain/motivation	○	○	○
Asking discovery questions about the current situation	○	○	○
Requesting detailed contact information	○	○	○
Discussing financing	○	○	○

Demonstrating the product	○	○	○
Using soft closes throughout the process	○	○	○
Tying the customer to one-of-a-kind	○	○	○
Handling price objections	○	○	○
Defusing the comments made by a competitor	○	○	○
Dealing with incentive requests and "value adds"	○	○	○
Negotiating prices	○	○	○
Asking for the sale	○	○	○
Asking for the sale a second time	○	○	○
Setting up a return visit	○	○	○
Following up by phone	○	○	○
Asking for referrals	○	○	○
Dealing with demanding customers	○	○	○
Making frequent calls to the customer after the sale	○	○	○
Responding to Internet leads	○	○	○
Using the CRM system	○	○	○
Handling paperwork	○	○	○
_____	○	○	○
_____	○	○	○
_____	○	○	○
_____	○	○	○
_____	○	○	○

How did that go? My hope is that the exercise was, well, uncomfortable. If you sailed through without a worry and finished in no time flat, with zero discomforts, you probably need to go back to page one and start over!

If you identified a large number of discomforts, don't be discouraged. Being honest in your self-assessment is a crucial first step in putting together an action plan.

GENERAL DISCOMFORTS

Of course, the principles I discuss in this book are not limited to sales discomforts. The fact is, you can apply these principles to your life in general. And as we all know, our lives "in general" greatly affect our vocational lives. With that in mind, here is a second list for you, this one dealing not with sales discomforts but with general life discomforts. I strongly encourage you to complete this chart as well, uncomfortable as it may be. (C'mon, you can do it! You eat discomfort for breakfast!)

For this list, simply put a check mark next to any of the discomforts in your life that you would rate "High" today:

- **Goal setting.** "I know I'm supposed to set goals, and I believe they could help me get more out of life. For whatever reason—lack of commitment, fear of failure, fear of success—I just don't do it."

- **Goal keeping.** "I am practically famous for setting aggressive goals, only to find myself giving up early in the game and working on other tasks."

- **Relationships.** "I have troubled relationships that need to be mended, and deep down I know that this means I have to confront my own faults and failings. But my excuses keep getting in the way of change."

- **Productivity.** "I get frustrated by the fact that I do not get more done, and I feel that if I worked smarter on the right things, I would be far more productive."

- **Service.** "I want to get involved in my community (whether it's charity, church, or society at large), but my discomfort keeps me from ever actually donating my time or resources."

- **Debt.** "I overspend. My lifestyle eats up every dollar I make—sometimes more. I have an insufficient amount of savings (or none at all). I know I could cut my budget, but I give in so easily to instant gratification."

- **Peer pressure.** "I think too much about what people think about me. I make too many decisions based on how I believe others will respond. I follow the crowd because it's comfortable. My sense of worth can tend to be based on what others think of me."

- **Confrontation.** "I avoid confrontation at all costs. At times I feel like a doormat, but it's just not worth the pain of an argument. I protect the status quo with coworkers, family members, even my own spouse."

- **Time management.** "I know I could be smarter in the way I use my time. There are opportunities for productivity that go untouched because I am 'busy' with unimportant tasks (TV, hobbies, video games, social media, and so on)."

- **Overcommitting.** "I have a hard time saying no. This could be based on a desire to please, an insecurity about my personal value, my tendency to micromanage, or any number of other reasons. My DIY approach to everything in life can be overwhelming."

- **Physical well-being.** "I know I need to eat right and to exercise, but junk food and channel surfing are so much more appealing. Besides, I can't stick with a diet or an exercise program when I start one, so why bother?"

- **Reading/growth.** "I've been meaning to finish this book I started, but I never seem to have the time. And yet I always seem to have time for TV. I could take a class at a community college or an online course, but that takes so much effort (much more effort than turning on my favorite reality show)."

- **Spiritual introspection.** "I don't spend time contemplating spiritual things. My theology is just strong enough to not nag at me, but I've never answered the question, 'What does God have to do with me, and what do I have to do with God?'"

- **Procrastination.** "I excel at putting off uncomfortable tasks, even when I know that doing so is at best counterproductive and at worst damaging to both my personal and my professional life. My tendencies toward procrastination eat at me constantly."

- **Temper issues.** "I have a tendency to lash out at people, even the people I love. I don't like it, but I feel a sense of control when I make people cower. I know it's something I need to change, but I'm not sure I'm capable of doing so."

- **Public speaking.** "I'd rather have a root canal than speak in front of a group. It's not that I think people will laugh out loud, but I fear that I will look stupid in front of them."

- **Other.** "It is not stated here, but I know my discomfort, and I know it well. It haunts me almost every day, and I cannot go on rationalizing why I put up with it. I struggle with ＿＿＿＿＿＿＿＿＿＿＿＿＿＿＿＿."

GETTING STARTED

Now that you have gone through and systematically evaluated your discomforts, I want to encourage you to do something right this minute: identify two discomforts, one major-league issue and another that is relatively minor.

Let's start with the beast. What is that gargantuan discomfort that you are not sure you will ever tame, the one that haunts you? Write that down in the following space.

My toughest and scariest discomfort is . . .

＿＿＿＿＿＿＿＿＿＿＿＿＿＿＿＿＿＿＿＿＿＿＿＿＿＿＿＿＿＿＿＿＿＿＿

＿＿＿＿＿＿＿＿＿＿＿＿＿＿＿＿＿＿＿＿＿＿＿＿＿＿＿＿＿＿＿＿＿＿＿

＿＿＿＿＿＿＿＿＿＿＿＿＿＿＿＿＿＿＿＿＿＿＿＿＿＿＿＿＿＿＿＿＿＿＿

I find this particularly frightening because . . .

_____

_____

_____

Well done. (We're on the honor system, but I'm trusting that you wrote something down!) We will circle back to the biggie in a short while. For now, let it be.

Now write down a discomfort from your list that you believe will be relatively easy to deal with. Find something that you rated as a low- or moderate-level discomfort.

One of my discomforts that should be easy to deal with is . . .

_____

_____

_____

Again, nicely done. We'll come back to this page in a little while. For now, try not to dwell on what you wrote down.

MOMENT OF DISCOMFORT . . . MOMENT OF DECISION

The sales discomforts you identified for yourself are both common and normal. In fact, those discomforts are probably part of your regular mental routine in the course of a sales week. Consciously or subconsciously, you know that they are out there, you anticipate their arrival, and you feel a familiar uneasiness when they show up. It is in those Moments of Discomfort that we experience a sensation in our gut, that familiar jab that triggers a twinge or a tweak . . . or maybe even genuine pain!

Personally, I have a physical response to moments of intense discomfort: I shudder. I do this weird whole-body-tenses-up thing when I face certain discomforts (taxes, needles, deadlines, even some phone calls). My wife will tell you that from time to time, she can actually see this reaction. If I'm lying in bed thinking when I should be sleeping, she will literally feel my stress as I suddenly shudder.

I want to reiterate that this book is not about eliminating discomfort, but rather about turning it into a productive opportunity. In fact, that Moment of Discomfort and the accompanying pain and anxiety it brings serve as very important signals of what will happen next. There is an inevitable and unavoidable progression already at work:

A Moment of Discomfort *always* leads to a Moment of Decision.

These two occurrences—the Moment of Discomfort and the Moment of Decision—are inseparable. Every discomfort begs for a decision, and the decision will be made in an instant. It is in these crucial moments that we are able to choose greatness.

THE DISCOMFORT DECISION

As a speaker and consultant, I am on the road more than I care to admit. Airports, taxis, and hotels are normal parts of my life, and I have found, over the years, that it is essential that I take care of myself if I want to stay healthy while I am on extended trips. That means that I must constantly face the discomfort of the Visit to the Hotel Gym. (Cue the spine-tingling music.)

I understand that many of the people who are reading this feel no discomfort whatsoever when it comes to working out, and good for you. For me, that's not the case. It's a chore, and it takes discipline. At the end of a long day on the road, what I really want to do is get horizontal with a remote control in my hand. But I know that the longer I put it off, the chance that I will actually work out becomes slimmer and slimmer (ironically). I need to exercise right away or it's just not going to happen. And so the moment I enter my hotel room and drop my stuff on the floor, I am faced with a discomfort. It's time. Right now. I am uncomfortable about working out, and that means I have a decision to make. How will I respond?

SALES DISCOMFORTS AND DECISIONS

How does that work for you? Think about your own Moments of Discomfort once again. At best, the norm is that we are barely aware of the internal dialogue that takes place during a Moment of Discomfort. Responses to discomfort are so habitual that it is likely that you may not recognize your own patterns of yielding in normal (that is, uncomfortable) sales moments. Consider these scenarios and the corresponding decisions that you are routinely faced with:

- "This customer looks really grumpy. Do I shake hands or not?"
- "She's asking for more money off the price. Do I give in on that?"
- "I have to make a difficult phone call. Is this a good time to update Facebook?"
- "It feels like it's time to ask for the order. Should I wait for him to ask me to purchase?"
- "I need to get this paperwork done. Can it wait?"
- "I promised my manager that I was going to practice a part of my demonstration out loud. Is that really necessary? Can I just say I did it?"
- "It's time to follow up on a stale lead. Maybe I'll give it another week and see if they call me."

Sound familiar? Do you recognize your own internal voice in any of those questions?

YOUR CHALLENGE

What are you learning about yourself during this evaluation process? What are you learning about your sales approach? About your presentation effectiveness? About your past frustrations? About your future success?

The reality is that the path of giving in to our discomfort is exceedingly dangerous, and the side effects are devastating:

- Burnout
- Identity crisis
- Lower than acceptable sales production
- Being viewed poorly by the company leaders
- Lack of confidence
- Ruts
- Poor self-esteem
- Lack of energy and enthusiasm
- Blaming or externalizing

That's a tough list, but it is entirely avoidable. I will soon show you an exact opposite list—the list of rewards that accompany being bold!

Questions to Ponder

- What struggles have you faced in life that made you stronger? Did you ever consider giving up? What kept you pressing forward?

- Recall a time when you practiced diligently to achieve a particular goal or acquire a skill. What motivated you to practice so hard? What feelings did you experience while you practiced? What feelings did you experience once you had achieved your goal or acquired that skill? Did you ever regret the effort you applied?

- As you completed the exercises in this chapter, did you discover any links between your sales discomforts and your general life discomforts? Is there any crossover?

- Will the same path perhaps enable you to dismantle both sets of discomforts? How can success in dealing with sales discomforts improve your ability to overcome general life discomforts and vice versa?

Now Try This . . .

1. My number one sales discomfort is:

   _____

2. *State of discomfort.* In the following space, use expressive words to describe your feelings when you are confronted with your number one sales discomfort:

   _____

   _____

   _____

   _____

3. *State of success.* Next, in this space, use equally expressive language to describe the feelings you have (or anticipate having) after you have boldly done the uncomfortable thing:

   _____

   _____

   _____

   _____

Now, when you are faced with a State of Discomfort in the coming days, replay in your mind the words and feelings you've associated with your State of Success. Propel yourself forward into those positive feelings by acting boldly. Let the obstacle become the path to true comfort.

Expert Interview: Rebecca Evans

Currently, there are 2.8 million sales professionals (internationally) doing business as independent beauty consultants for Mary Kay Cosmetics. A handful of them have worked their way up to the position of national sales director. How good must these few be!

Rebecca Evans's journey to becoming an independent senior national sales director is a story of overcoming the odds; she could be a poster child for how to deal with comfort addiction. Today she speaks at conferences internationally, mentors other consultants around the world, and in her spare time runs her own thriving business.

Tell me about your journey. How did you get started selling Mary Kay in the first place?

I come from a big family. I was the only girl, and I had seven brothers. It was brutal in my house at times, and I learned the need to be assertive from an early age.

My passion as a young woman was for broadcasting, and I pursued a career in radio. I loved my work and thought it was what I would do forever. I worked for a lot of small radio stations doing sales, PR, voice-overs, and some on-air stuff. It was a slow career progression, and over time, I realized that I wouldn't be content making that work my lifelong pursuit.

And that's when you fell in love with Mary Kay?

It wasn't Mary Kay ... I fell in love with the idea of making a difference in people's lives. To be honest, Mary Kay was just a way to make some extra money.

Being a salesperson for Mary Kay felt like the right fit pretty quickly, but it took a solid year for me to learn the ropes. When my personal life fell into place after starting work for Mary Kay, it was my confirmation that I was in the right career. I've now been at Mary Kay for thirty-one years.

Was it success at first sight?

Not even close, actually. It was pretty clear after my first year that this was something I was meant to do, but it took me a while to get any traction.

Up to that point, the biggest thing missing in my professional life was a mentor. I really needed mentoring, especially from women. (I didn't get that in the radio industry.) I cannot say enough about how important it is to have mentors to guide you along the way and keep you on track.

Tell me about the early days at Mary Kay. Describe the first year.

I was pretty uncomfortable most of the time. But I had grown up in an uncomfortable environment, and the lack of relational coddling from my brothers had prepared me well for dealing with discomfort head-on.

That said, the early discomfort at Mary Kay was pretty painful, actually. I had a lousy complexion, and I just didn't look like I belonged in the cosmetics industry. I was not confident, and it showed.

True story: I wore the standard Mary Kay badge that we all had back then, but I used to cover it up with the wide strap of my purse for fear that someone would actually approach me and want to ask a question!

Did you almost quit?

I probably quit a dozen times in the first year or so. More accurately, I fired myself several times. But I got some good advice early on: "Keep your calendar filled with activities." I really tried to keep my schedule filled up with anything I could find that might afford me the opportunity to talk about Mary Kay. If I had an especially lousy day, it helped to have something on the calendar for the next day. I found that hope was a powerful motivator.

Do some salespeople just have the "it" factor? Or is sales success something that is learned over time?

I don't think there are born salespeople; I think there are born people people. It comes down to a matter of who is willing to be uncomfortable. Who is willing to practice the presentation? Who is willing to get it wrong before they get it right? I think sales is like most everything else in life. If you want to get it right, you have to roll up your sleeves and work hard. That's the part that trips a lot of people up.

A big part of success in sales is based on prospecting for new business. Which is tougher, in your opinion: generating a new lead or closing the sale with the lead you have?

I think I would have to say closing the lead in front of me. I am a relational person, and I like to help people, so telling someone about Mary Kay is not difficult for me. The products and the company changed my life, and I know it can do the same for them. The telling is the easier part; the closing is the harder part.

What is the secret to finding "humble boldness"?

I always try to follow the platinum rule: "Treat others the way they want to be treated." It's not about me. It's about serving the customer in front of me. Backing off and hiding behind my own fears is hardly a service.

Did you ever meet the great Mary Kay Ash?

I did, many years ago. And from the start, I bought into her mission. I was all in right from the beginning. In those early days, when I was struggling so much, I just couldn't give up on her. I had aligned myself with her message and her direction. I went to my first convention and found myself totally immersed in her approach, which was scriptural. The main tenets of Mary Kay's mission were: follow the Golden Rule; honest pay for honest work; consider one another's interests ahead of your own; God first, family second, career third.

She was an amazing lady.

Story Time
Rationalizations and Other Bad Habits

The most pernicious aspect of procrastination is that it can become a habit. We don't just put off our lives today; we put them off till our deathbed.

—Steven Pressfield

THE BIG IDEA
Rationalizations are success killers.

So far, we have determined that every Moment of Discomfort is accompanied by a Moment of Decision, and that these moments are simultaneous, inevitable, and unavoidable. We have also established that the decision to be made can be boiled down to a simple choice: will I do the bold (although uncomfortable) thing, or will I give in to my desire for comfort and find an easier path?

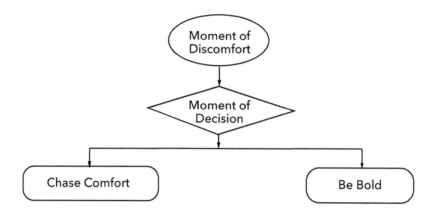

Suppose you have been working with a prospect for some time and everything is going well. Of course there have been obstacles, but your sales mastery has turned them into nonissues. The demonstration was as good as it gets—clearly your performance would qualify as a future management training tool if this happened to be a secret shopper. Yes, the price was a concern but your demonstration skills in building value were so stellar that the client is practically begging to pay more than list price. You get the picture.

At some moment of high drama in the process, during a very slight pause in the conversation, a voice in the back of your head whispers loudly, "This would be a good time to ask for the sale."

Do you know the voice? Have you experienced such a moment? In my experience, "the voice" is a common phenomenon that virtually every sales professional is familiar with. It comes upon us in an instant, often taking us by surprise. The voice is very, very real.

The important question is: How do you respond?

My hope is that you heed that voice and act on its instruction. It is clearly time for a closing question. But what if you are dealing with significant discomfort at that very moment? What if self-doubt creeps up simultaneously and causes you to question whether asking for the sale is the right thing to do? And what if you give in to that second voice that says, "No, wait for them to ask you if they can purchase." What happens now?

Let's explore.

HOW DO WE SLEEP AT NIGHT?

Remember Neck Pillow Guy? Do you recall his tendency to walk back and forth but never actually talk to anyone, constantly avoiding conversations because he was so uncomfortable? Here's what I was thinking as I watched him for more than five minutes: "How does this guy live with himself?" I mean, the guy needs to be able to sleep at night, doesn't he? How does he do it?

When we give in to our discomfort and take the easy path (for example, when we ignore the voice that tells us to ask for the sale—or even to approach someone in a mall), there is a kind of internal compass that kicks in and sends a message that our actions are off-track. We know we are supposed to ask for the sale, and when we choose not to, we take one more step down the easy path—the well-worn route of our addiction to comfort.

We typically know when we are giving into our addiction to comfort—our conscience makes that clear—but we still don't want to face up to that discomfort. We don't have it in us to say, "Yup, I'm yielding right now." And yet we have to live with ourselves. We have to find a quick, clever, and convenient way to get out of the mental consequences of giving in to the discomfort. How do we do this?

I believe that our moral compass demands an answer—a justification for our actions—and we are very quick to oblige in the form of rationalizations.

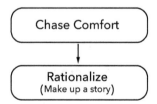

I call this step in the process "making up stories," and it is a skill that we have developed into a fine art over the course of our lives.

Neck Pillow Guy has some very common (and I daresay overused) stories at the ready for every one of his give-in moments:

- "They don't have any money. Look how they're dressed."
- "She's walking too fast. People who walk at that speed won't stop to talk to me."
- "He looks mean. And I've learned that only nice people buy my product."
- "Too young."
- "Too old."
- "This won't fit around his neck."

Stories. All stories. And all easily conjured up for his own mental self-protection.

If I had a dime for every salesperson who has ever told me, "No one wants to be called at home," I would be very, very wealthy. For business-to-consumer sales, calls to the home phone have always been considered a standard practice. Yet many salespeople swear, "No one wants to be called at home."

I believe this is a story, a rationalization. After all, no one wants to be called at home? *No one?* There are seven billion people on the planet. Not one of them wants to be called at home?

Of course, this is simply not true. If your best friend called you at home, you wouldn't mind, would you? And what is the difference here? It is simply a matter of the depth of the relationship. Is it possible that the salesperson in question is really saying, "No one wants *me* to call them at home"? That is a different issue altogether!

THE SCIENCE OF RATIONALIZATIONS

Take any freshman psychology class and you'll learn a great deal about rationalizations. You will find them categorized under the heading of "thinking errors," and that is an appropriate classification. We come across a perceived threat, and we immediately seek a mental justification for why we should not act. Psychologists offer a slew of types of rationalizing, or what Zig Ziglar would have called "stinkin' thinkin'":

- Catastrophizing (making mountains out of molehills)
- Mind reading (assuming the worst in a prospect's thinking)
- Overgeneralizing (making broad decisions based upon sparse experience)
- Labeling (jumping to conclusions about whom to work with)
- Mental filtering (seeing what you want to see)
- Personalizing (thinking it's all about you)

All of these (and many more such thinking errors) fall into the category of "negative automatic thoughts." However, they are only as automatic as we have allowed them to be—or even trained them to be—over time. They are distortions of reality. They appear valid at a given moment, but they are just plain wrong.

> *Rationalizations give us a comfortable place, a shelter from the winds of the sales process.*

These thinking errors provide us with the illusion of safety. We can hide behind what seems to be a legitimate rationale. Indeed, you can choose to do just that . . . as long as you are prepared to endure the consequence: chronic under-performance. Rationalizations give us a comfortable place, a shelter from the winds of the sales process. However, it has been said, and rightly so, that "a ship is safe in its harbor . . . but that is not what ships were built for" (anonymous).

The problem is that our thinking errors occur instinctively. A lot of what we call thinking takes place in the dark and subconscious regions of our brains. Many of our cognitive patterns are hardwired into our DNA, providing protective instructions to deal with threatening situations. These "automatic thoughts" are just that—automatic. As Malcolm Gladwell (in *Blink*) writes, "What we think of as free will is largely an illusion: much of the time, we are simply operating on automatic pilot, and the way we think and act—and *how well* we think and act on the spur of the moment—are a lot more susceptible to outside influences than we realize."

This automatic pilot mode can keep us alive in some situations—when we hear a rattle coming from a bush while we are on a hike, for example, or when someone enters a bank wearing a mask. It is when our sensitivity to threats is overemployed in situations that are not necessarily threatening that we get into trouble. In a sales conversation, our brains will often take a common discomfort and inflate it into a full-blown threat to our well-being. It happens on a deep psychological level, but it is a very real occurrence. And the effects are crippling to a salesperson's success.

MAKING UP STORIES: THE DOWNSIDE OF CREATIVITY

Psychologists have all kinds of fancy terminology for the things we tell ourselves. I call them what they are: stories. They are convenient mental fallbacks that provide us with protection from our discomforts. Our stories are self-protective mechanisms that allow us to accept lower-quality decisions, yet still be able to live with ourselves. They act as a mental construct for our rationalizations.

Typically, the stories are externally based, allowing us to place the rationalizing factor on someone or something other than ourselves (psychologists consider this to be part of "attribution theory"). Recall Neck Pillow Guy and some of his stories:

- "They don't have any money. Look how they're dressed."

- "She's walking too fast. People who walk at that speed won't stop to talk to me."

- "He looks mean. And I've learned that only nice people buy my product."

Note that all the stories are about the prospect, not about the salesperson. Attribution theory states that if I externalize the situation, I can remove myself from a position of culpability for my otherwise self-destructive behaviors. What we end up with is the proverbial sour grapes story: "It's not me; it's you."

STORYTELLING IN REAL TIME

When my daughter, Katie, was 16, she had this "thing" for a young man we'll call Robert. One summer afternoon, Robert was at our house for a little video gaming in the family room.

> *Rationalization is a process not of perceiving reality,*
> *but of attempting to make reality fit one's emotions.*
>
> —Ayn Rand

Now, you might think I'm from Mars when I say this, but we always had a "no physical contact" rule in our house. (For the record, the rule did not apply to my wife and me!) As I walked through the family room that day, I noticed something that rocked me. Katie and Robert were sitting on the sofa playing a video game, and I noticed that (gasp!) their knees were touching!

How uncomfortable was this? Did I really want to be the kind of father who would make a scene over a house rule violation? Was I going to pull out a ruler and insist on a six-inch separation? How uncomfortable would Katie be? Or Robert? Or me!

I decided that the discomfort was beyond my ability to handle. I simply could not pull the trigger and deal with the situation. I kept walking.

Think back to the progression:

1. Moment of Discomfort

2. Moment of Decision

3. Give in to the discomfort

4. What happens next?

Do you remember Step 4? Yep, I had to make up a story. It was not a difficult task. After all, I had become quite adept at this instantaneous creative art form.

"You know what? They're playing a video game, and they are really into it. They probably don't even realize their knees are touching."

Wait. Why are you snickering at that? Oh, I get it. You were 16 once. And when you were, did you realize when your knees were touching? Uh, yeah! I don't know about you, but for me it was part of a 45-minute strategy to get to the point where my knee was touching hers!

Do you see how easy and simple and natural this is? As we go through life, we become so good at our storytelling that we end up having stories that we are not even aware of. Telling ourselves stories becomes second nature. It is a (seemingly) comfortable and normal state of being.

COMMON SALES STORIES (WHAT ARE YOURS?)

Over the years, I have become something of an expert on the stories that salespeople tell. Some of them are from my own experience. Others I hear over and over again from salespeople everywhere.

I was working with the members of a home builder's sales team in Las Vegas and confronting them about a common problem—not asking for the sale on the prospect's first visit to the community. I was stressing the need to shorten the buying cycle by setting up the closing question earlier in the process.

During this portion of the sales training, a gentleman sitting to my immediate right had a posture that said (screamed, actually), "I ain't buyin' what you're sellin'!" His body language was clearly negative, and there was no doubt that he did not accept the premise of my discussion.

After a while, he raised his hand. His attitude was obvious as he asked his question: "You know, all those people who bought on visit one—how many of them canceled the order later on?" Then he sat back with a smug look on his face, as if to say, "Caught you on that one, trainer guy. What do you have to say now?"

Evaluate this with me. What was really going on here? What was this salesperson communicating? Here are a couple of observations from my perspective:

1. This salesperson was scared to death to ask for the sale on the first visit.

2. This salesperson needed to justify why he did not do so.

3. This salesperson came up with a very convenient story to rationalize his actions.

(By the way, here was my response: "I don't know the statistical answer to your question. I do know that the chances that a customer will actually complete a purchase increase when he or she signs a contract." In other words, maybe these customers will cancel the sale and maybe they won't. But I'll take my 50 percent cancellation rate on my four sales over your 0 percent cancellation rate on zero sales any day of the week. Do the math!)

I'll share some of the more common stories that are conjured up in a salesperson's mind, but I'd like you to do more than just read them; I want you to try them on for size. Be honest and ask yourself whether you have heard these stories in your own head. Consider writing in the margins or simply checking off some of the stories you are familiar with.

- **Engaging the prospect:** "People don't want to engage with a salesperson. They just want to be left alone."

- **Exchanging names:** "People don't want to exchange names. That's too aggressive early on."

- **Shaking hands:** "People aren't comfortable with shaking hands too early."

- **Dealing with people who are curt, rude, or even mean:** "He was rude first. I don't have to take that."

- **Asking the motivation question:** "People don't want to share that with me. It's too personal."

- **Asking discovery questions:** "I don't want to come off as nosy."

- **Discussing financing:** "That's too personal" or "It's too early."

- **Demonstrating the product:** "The customers know what they want. My product sells itself."

- **Soft closes:** "They'll let me know if they like it. I can tell without having to ask."
- **Price objections:** "I'll ruin the relationship if I come off as defensive."
- **Product objections:** "No one likes _____."
- **Dealing with incentive requests or negotiations:** "I don't want them to think I'm hiding anything."
- **Asking for the sale:** "People will let me know when they're ready to buy."
- **Asking for the sale a second time:** "That's just too pushy. I'll offend them."
- **Asking for a second appointment:** "It will be easier for them if they call me."
- **Following up by phone:** "People prefer e-mail."
- **Asking for referrals:** "If we do our job, we don't have to ask."
- **Practicing:** "Role playing isn't real life—it doesn't help things."
- **Getting outsold:** "I lost the sale to a competitor who is giving away the farm."

Now, you may be thinking, "Hey, but that's not a story; it's true. My competitor really is giving away the farm!" Allow me to clarify this point. There is a kernel of truth in every single statement you just read. The key here is to distinguish where that kernel of truth ends and your imagination begins. How much are you relying on these stories to justify unhealthy sales behavior?

Here's an example: dealing with mean people. Some salespeople do just fine in dealing with people who are curt, rude, or even mean. Others crumble. The salesperson who struggles in that situation is, of course, unlikely to win the sale. He or she will appease or even patronize the customer and (subconsciously) work to put an end to the painful conversation as quickly as possible.

Suppose the customer leaves without having even hinted at purchasing. Now the sales manager comes along to ask about the interaction, and the salesperson responds, "That guy was just downright mean. We wouldn't even want him as a customer here." All is well—we can move on with our lives.

> *Comfort-driven salespeople will create such a believable story that they will never know the possible outcome.*

But hold on a moment. Was the customer really mean? Perhaps he was just plain afraid. And if he was afraid, could that fear have been based upon the fact that he was seriously considering a purchase, but he felt that he had been abused by a salesperson in the past? The problem is that comfort-driven salespeople will create such believable stories that they will never know the possible outcome. They will simply move on to the next (hopefully nicer) prospect.

GENERAL DISCOMFORT STORIES

While we are focusing this discussion on discomfort as it relates to the world of sales, discomfort and storytelling are not, of course, limited to that arena. The fact is that storytelling is a part of our day-to-day lives. Take a moment and see if you can relate to some of these common life discomfort stories.

- **Goal setting:** "That's for those really driven people. I'm more spontaneous."
- **Goal keeping:** "A new goal has come along that is more important."
- **Relationships:** "I know I've handled it poorly, but she has done worse than I have."
- **Productivity:** "I do as much as or maybe more than a lot of people."
- **Service:** "Other people will sign up."
- **Debt:** "I owe it to myself."
- **Peer pressure:** "I will be a better friend if I go along with this group."

- **Confrontation:** "I'll cause an even bigger scene if I say something now."

- **Time management:** "My schedule is much more open tomorrow."

- **Overcommitting:** "If you want something done right, you have to do it yourself."

- **Physical well-being:** "It's just one cookie (mocha, slice of pizza, soda, or whatever."

- **Reading/growth:** "I can't fit that class into my schedule."

- **Spiritual introspection:** "I go to church from time to time; that's enough."

- **Procrastination:** "I don't even know where to start. I'll look at this later."

- **Public speaking:** "I don't have anything to say that anyone would want to hear."

WHAT ARE YOUR STORIES?

This is a difficult portion of the book because it requires something important of you: brutal honesty. It is much easier to see the stories and tendencies in the people around us, but the magic happens when we identify those stories within ourselves. And this happens only when we are willing to be honest.

So think back on a recent sales encounter that did not go your way and ask yourself these questions:

- What was the discomfort?
- What happened that caused you to yield?
- How did you feel?
- What were your choices?
- How did you respond?
- What would the bold move have looked like?

- Which path did you take?
- If you yielded to your discomfort, what story did you tell?
- How naturally did your story come to you?
- How did you feel afterward?
- How do you feel now about the encounter?

The purpose here is not to make you feel bad about your presentation. If anything, you should feel excited. Knowing what it takes to overcome your own barriers is a barrier removed! The beauty is that you can take the concepts you will learn in this book and carry them into your next conversation.

Take two minutes to write down a common story that you tell yourself in the space given here. Be honest; having the confidence to acknowledge your stories is a powerful step in your growth:

_____

_____

_____

_____

_____

_____

_____

_____

_____

THE POWER OF THE REWRITE

And that leads us to the good news, the exciting news. The stories that you tell, the juicy rationalizations—they don't have to remain in place. You have the power to rewrite them. The best way to dismantle your stories is to recognize them in advance. Then you can replace them with powerful positive stories based on your new beliefs. After doing this, when you face the discomfort, you will already know what to say, and your mental conversation will be based on a paradigm of success and confidence.

I'll show you how to rewrite your stories in Part II of this book. For now, take comfort in the fact that you can control your response to every single discomfort you face in the sales arena!

THE TOUCHIEST "STORY"

Before moving on, I want to address one particularly difficult story that trips up many a sales professional. I often ask salespeople to define their role in the sales process. The answers I get range from "provide information that will help clients make a decision" to "serve the clients in their best interests" to "shepherd the clients through the buying process." I very rarely hear the more blunt answer: "convince them to purchase from me."

The word *convince* can cause many salespeople tremendous angst. It is often associated with the word *pushy*, and *no one* wants to be pushy, right? Pushy is exactly what our mothers told us not to be. "Jeff, don't be pushy. Nobody likes pushy people."

It turns out that this adage has stuck with us into adulthood. Dan Pink (*To Sell Is Human*) points to a study he conducted in which he asked people for the first word that came to mind when they thought of "selling." The number one adjective was "pushy."

Let's rethink that for a moment.

Suppose there is a sliding glass door in the sales environment in which you work, and also suppose that you have seen more than one person walk right into that door. Now suppose you are working with a customer who is about to do the exact same thing. You have only enough time to reach out and physically halt your customer's progress.

If you want to take your mother's advice and not be pushy, the conversation will sound something like this:

Now, before you proceed even one step more, I need to tell you that it is my job to give you all the information you need in order to make an intelligent decision. I cannot decide for you, but I would like to review the pros and cons of taking one more step. Shall I?

Is that how you would respond? No! You would physically and forcefully intervene in a relatively aggressive manner. Quick question: Are you being pushy in your behavior? Of course you are, and literally so!

The more important question is this: Are you acting appropriately? Your instinct probably says, "Yes, that is appropriate behavior." Why? What makes that an appropriate way to respond to the situation? The obvious answer: because it is in your customer's best interest. And that is the key takeaway.

> *There are times when pushy or aggressive or assertive behavior will be in the customer's best interest, and it would be just plain wrong to act in any other manner.*

There are times when pushy or aggressive or assertive (whatever you want to call it) behavior will be in the customer's best interest, and it would be just plain wrong to act in any other manner. Suppose a customer is seriously considering purchasing from a competitor who is offering a lower price, but you know in your heart that it would be a tremendous mistake for this customer to do so. In this case, you have a moral obligation to be pushy.

PUSHY STORIES

Remember, when we yield in those uncomfortable situations and take the easy path, our moral compass warns us that we are making a mistake. That's when the stories pop up in order to justify our actions.

Perhaps you will recognize some stories that are centered on being pushy:

- "I'm not one of those hard-sell salespeople."
- "I prefer relationship selling."
- "If I'm pushy, I'll destroy everything I've worked for."
- "They won't like me if I push too hard."
- "My mother told me not to be pushy."

Again, each of those statements might be true to some extent in some situations, so we have to go back and look at our qualifier. The question to ask is: "What action of mine is in the customer's best interest?"

The reality is that the stories are simply ways of masking the true discomfort:

- "I am scared to death of how I might be perceived."
- "What customers think of me matters more to me than making a sale."
- "Asking for the sale scares the crap out of me."
- "I get the shakes when it's time to make phone calls."
- "I feel as if my career will fall apart if I make a single wrong move. (Better safe than sorry!)"

THE DARK JOURNEY OF REPEATED STORIES

Let's review:

1. The stories are always there whenever we give in to our desire for comfort.
2. The stories are believable, and we believe them.
3. Though the stories could be true in some circumstances, most of the time they are made up for our mental convenience.

Pay attention to that third statement because in that truth, you will find some really good news. If you can make up rationalization stories, you can also make up brand-new and far more productive stories! (We'll address this in great detail in Part II of the book.)

On the other hand, if you choose to continue to believe your rationalization stories, you will find that this is a path that takes a dark and damaging turn. Before I journey into the remedy for all this, I want to touch briefly on the consequences of continuing to yield. I will show you the long-term effects of repeated storytelling in the next chapter. Fair warning: they ain't pretty.

I suspect that in this chapter, I have challenged your thinking in some fairly intense ways. By now you may be feeling some uneasiness or even dread about all this. I want to encourage you to embrace that feeling of uncertainty, for in it you will find a path to a very necessary change. Call it "creative destruction," the process of dismantling long-held mental structures in favor of new and better fortresses. You might be experiencing what psychologists call *cognitive dissonance*, which means that you are feeling a little (or a lot) lost. If this is where you find yourself right now, consider it a good thing.

Questions to Ponder

- Can you relate to the voice that prompts you to ask for the sale? Can you also relate to the competing voice that prompts you to yield and not ask for it? Think back to a selling situation in which you heard both voices—how did you respond? What motivated you to make that decision? What can you learn and apply from that motivation?

- Take a moment to reflect on the thoughts and feelings that you experienced as you read the section about the stories that we tell ourselves. Did you immediately connect personally with some stories that you tell yourself? If you didn't, take the time right now to dig deeper and uncover your own stories. This critical step will enable you to rewrite those stories later in the book.

- How do you feel about the concept of "pushiness"? Have you found yourself rationalizing ways to avoid pushiness, even when it might serve your client's best interests? Have you ever lost a sale because you felt uncomfortable about asserting yourself? If so, whose interests were you serving most—your own or the client's?

Now Try This . . .

This week, make a concerted effort to *catch yourself telling stories*. As the book progresses, you will begin rewriting your stories, but for now, just develop the habit of listening for and identifying the stories. This will help you enhance your sensitivity to each and every Moment of Decision. Use the simple table given here to track how many times each day you catch yourself telling stories during the current week.

Monday	Tuesday	Wednesday	Thursday	Friday

Expert Interview: Nancy Ancowitz

Often, the words *bold* and *introvert* are thought of as mutually exclusive. This is a myth. Moreover, this myth suggests that introverts simply do not have what it takes to be effective sales professionals. Nancy Ancowitz strongly disagrees.

Ancowitz is a business communication coach and teaches presentation skills and business writing courses at New York University. She is the author of the seemingly enigmatic book: *Self-Promotion for Introverts*® (a very strongly recommended read, by the way). Her blog posts at selfpromotionforintroverts .com are interesting, funny, and challenging.

Nancy, I'm writing about boldness in the face of discomfort, knowing that many people see boldness as the opposite of introversion. Do you agree?

The opposite of boldness is wimpiness, which does not define introversion— unless you think the abilities to think deeply, listen deeply, and form deep relationships are hallmarks of a wimp. Put simply, introverts are deep-sea divers to extroverts' snorkelers. If you're an introvert, typically you're more detail oriented, attracted to activities that take prolonged focus, such as research, and prefer the company of one person at a time to large group interactions.

Introversion and extroversion are functions of what fuels you. Are you naturally more energized by quietly doing one thing at a time or multitasking amid a constant buzz? If you're an introvert, you are more often energized by looking inward ("intro") as opposed to reaching outward ("extro"). That's not a function of how bold you are. In fact, an introvert can boldly go after business—however, her often more cerebral approach is different from an extrovert's.

You may be surprised that introverts make up half the population—we're just the quieter half. So there's nothing wrong with you if you're an introvert. To dispel another common misconception, introversion shouldn't be confused with shyness, or social anxiety, which can be overcome through psychotherapy and other types of self-discovery and support. Introversion, on the other hand, is not curable—and I hope you can see that it's not a malady.

Can an introvert be an effective salesperson?

Without a doubt! Introverts often have an advantage at selling. They thoroughly research a prospect, network behind the scenes to link to helpful contacts and gather useful "intel," and connect best with their prospects individually.

Talk about introverts who have a high achievement drive. Some would suggest that the very idea is an oxymoron.

The idea that introverts aren't driven is folly—a silly stereotype. Forty percent of CEOs are introverts. Theirs is often a more reflective leadership. Think Warren Buffett. I wrote *Self-Promotion for Introverts*® to help introverts build the skills and create the strategies that they need to get where they want in their careers. If you're an introvert, you'll do that by using your quieter assets, rather than exhausting yourself by trying to act like an extrovert.

So it's a silly stereotype, but one that is widely held. Does this affect the self-perception of introverts?

The stereotype makes it difficult for some introverts—especially ones growing up in households and communities that drown them out and don't value their quieter contributions. As adults, introverts who work in organizations that reward nonstop interaction, hobnobbing, and lots of unscheduled meetings with frequent brainstorming may feel marginalized for not quite fitting in.

Can you give me an example of how that problem manifests itself?

Some introverts question themselves in ways that raise doubts about their worth. We see this in a phenomenon called "impostor syndrome." If you suffer from that, you harbor an irrational fear that others will discover that you are not as smart, talented, or competent as you might appear—and that your wins were just an accident. I recently interviewed Dr. Stephen Brookfield on this subject, for my blog. He suggested that if you struggle with impostor syndrome, you are convinced that you are the only person who is not "up to the job." Once you've convinced yourself of this "fact," your self-doubt can take on a life of its own.

Your book, *Self-Promotion for Introverts®*, is full of charts and lists and exercises. Tell me your thought process in developing that material.

I wrote the book with an appreciation that we learn in different ways. So I provided a variety of materials—advice, anecdotes, interviews, charts, tables, checklists—to offer alternative ways to look at different information. And for introverts, who tend to have the patience to do a deeper dive into a topic, in search of a more detailed understanding, I provided plenty of room for discovery. My extrovert readers can integrate the information in their own ways—for example, socializing it and brainstorming at a cocktail party about the ideas I've shared.

Is introversion inspired by nature or nurture?

I believe you're born either an introvert or an extrovert. And we're all complex human beings with many aspects to our personalities. So you can be an introvert who is highly sociable at times (like me) or a pensive extrovert who loves long nature walks. To me, the more compelling question is how to harness your energy and strengths to get what you want in your career. Whether you're more of a Garbo in a cubicle or a social butterfly, the keys are to both recognize your natural inclinations and authentically use your gifts. Do that, and there's no limit to how much you can sell.

The Gut Check
Where Discomfort Leads and What Is at Stake

Discomfort is very much a part of my master plan.

—Jonathan Lethem

THE BIG IDEA
Your standards are not what you desire; they are what you accept.

By now I hope you have identified some significant discomforts in your sales life. There is one more discovery you need to make, and it has to do with the "reward" for following the comfortable path. Be forewarned: the consequences are more dire than you may be expecting.

I'll share a story that I believe puts everything we've discussed into a real-world scenario. See if you can identify your own tendencies in this situation.

Several years ago my wife and I were heading out for a quick bite to eat at a nearby Chipotle. I had my hand on the restaurant door when out of nowhere I heard a woman's voice say, "Excuse me, do you have any money? I want to buy some food."

No doubt you have experienced an awkward moment like this. Is that situation uncomfortable for anyone besides me? Perhaps you have no problem at all with such scenarios. You might have absolutely zero discomfort when this situation arises in your life, but I confess that for me, such occurrences put me far outside of my comfort zone.

You may think ill of me when you hear how I respond, but I'm the guy who is going to softly but abruptly say, "No." Then I'll keep on walking. I need to get away from that discomfort as fast as possible.

When I'm faced with this kind of situation, I make the decision to give in to my discomfort, and I go down the easy path. Of course, you know what happens next, don't you? What follows in the progression? Moment of Discomfort, Moment of Decision, give in to discomfort, go down the easy path, and . . . make up a story. That's right, I have to make up a story in order to rationalize my behavior.

In this case, my mental story is simple: "You're just going to buy drugs." Continuing that story, my mind suggests, "My not giving you money means that you cannot buy drugs, and the whole of society is better off because of my noble action in this situation!" Do you see how juicy and creative this rationalization tendency is in our lives?

Let me be clear that I am not espousing simply handing out cash to everyone who asks for it. The situation for me is actually a great deal more complex than that. If it were just a matter of handing over a buck or two, it would be easy. The real discomfort comes from the nagging feeling that I should be talking to this person. Just handing over the money falls into the "give a man a fish" classification. But if I am to "teach a man to fish," it means that I have to get involved on some level. I can't handle that—it's too far outside my comfort zone.

My wife, Karen, is much bolder than I in such situations. In this case, she turned to the lady and said, "Of course. We're at a restaurant. Come on in and let me buy you dinner."

The lady was clearly taken aback by this response. She hesitated for a brief moment before saying, "Oh, well, actually it's for my kids. They're in a motel room up the street."

Karen replied, "Not a problem. I'll buy food for you and your children. They can wrap it up to go. C'mon in."

The lady paused again, clearly frustrated. "Well, I wouldn't want it to get cold."

Karen responded, "You know what? If they are that hungry, I don't think they'll mind."

The lady turned around and walked away.

What do you think? Well handled? I think so! I was both impressed and humbled by how calmly and rationally Karen dealt with the situation. For her, this occurrence was just not that far outside her comfort zone. Her heart instructs her to reach out to people in situations like this.

Fast-forward 12 hours.

The very next morning, I was in Stockton, California, to speak at a conference. On my way to breakfast, I stopped to buy a newspaper out of a rack in front of a grocery store. At the moment I was reaching for the paper, I heard a man's voice, out of nowhere, saying to me, "Do you have any money? I'm hungry."

Now, you know me. I would normally blow this guy off, right? Again, my story is already in place: "Get a job and you can buy your own food." But just hours earlier, Karen had role-modeled my response to this situation. This will be easy, right? I am well prepared to school this guy.

I turned around and confidently said to the young man, "No problem. The store has a deli and a bakery. Come on in and I'll buy you some food." I was smug and a bit cocky. I was rather looking forward to the battle that was about to ensue.

The young man was quiet for several awkward moments before stuttering this response: "Would . . . would you do . . . do that for me? I haven't eaten in two days."

Whoa! Needless to say, that was *not* the response I was anticipating. I was stunned. And what do you think was going through my mind at that point? Well, to be honest, my first thought was, "Dude, did you not read the script? That was *not* how this was supposed to go down. You were supposed to argue with me, and I had some snappy retorts all lined up."

What was I to do? I had offered, and he had accepted. The next thing I knew, I was walking a young man named Adrian through a Safeway grocery store to buy him some food.

Quick question: where is my discomfort now? It is off the charts!

I confess that I really did not want to be there, but as I was walking Adrian through the store, it became clear to me that my initial story was not going to work after all. "Get a job and you can buy your own food"? Not Adrian. Adrian was not put together right. He was "not all there" mentally, and it was clear that no one was going to give him a job. Adrian had fallen through a crack in the system, and it became very clear to me what was happening: either I feed Adrian or Adrian goes hungry.

I bought him some food and gave him what little money I had on me so that he could have a second meal later in the day.

How do you suppose I was feeling at this point? Pleased? Satisfied? Happy to have helped? Yes, all of the above, as a matter of fact. I experienced all those sentiments . . . and one more. I immediately felt powerfully convicted, asking myself this question: "All right, Shore, how many people has God placed in your path and said, 'Feed this person,' but they went hungry because you were more concerned about being comfortable?"

Chew on that one for a moment, will you? I've been chewing on it for years.

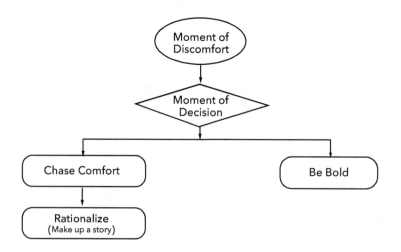

WHO IS THIS BOOK REALLY FOR?

Throughout this book, I have referred to our areas of discomfort and our tendencies toward going down the easy path. But I have spent little time on the main character: your customer. You must understand that this entire discussion is not really about you, at least not primarily. Your addiction to comfort is not a victimless crime!

When we ignore our responsibility to boldly act as a persuasive advisor to our customers, we force them to act solely on their own.

I often wonder how many customers have unknowingly settled for their car, their jewelry, their insurance policy, or their home, thinking that these purchases were "right" for them. When we ignore our responsibility to boldly act as a persuasive advisor to our customers, we force them to act solely on their own. And if we are forcing them to act on their own, why are we even there?

Giving in to your discomfort benefits neither you nor your company, but the real loser here is the customer, who desperately needs your bold direction during the sales process. Your customers need your help. Will you be there for them?

Back in the day, I sold homes—hundreds of homes, as a matter of fact. I loved it. I changed people's worlds in a very significant way. I made a huge impact on their lives. How cool is that?

But every now and then I would get a bombshell—I would lose a valued customer to a competitor. I am a very competitive individual, and I don't like to lose. But to lose the sale and to know that a customer had bought a home that wasn't right for her . . . that killed me!

Early in my sales career, I was overly concerned with the idea that I might damage my relationships with my customers if I came across as pushy. The idea of being assertive was distasteful to me, and I told myself that I was serving my customers most appropriately by letting them make their own decisions in their own time.

Later I learned that trusted advisors are persuasive people, and that they assertively press their customers to do things that are in the customers' best interests. If I knew that a customer was considering purchasing a home that had a lower price but was not the right home for that individual, I had a moral obligation to step in and say what needed to be said. It would have been just plain indecent of me to allow that customer to purchase the wrong home without saying anything about the decision.

A CASE STUDY IN "PUSHINESS"

When I was the national sales director at a Fortune 500 company, I was invited to attend a VIP lunch that was being held at the House of Blues on Sunset Boulevard in Hollywood. I had never been to this venue, but I imagined that it could qualify as the hippest place on the planet.

This may come as a huge surprise, but it has been a very long time since anyone accused me of being hip. I was totally at sea as I tried to figure out what hip would look like at the House of Blues. I was guessing $400 jeans, a turtleneck, and flip-flops. What did I know?

I made my way to Nordstrom, not because it's the hippest place on the planet, but because I believed I could trust the salespeople to understand my plight. The salesman assembled an outfit: black slacks, merino wool sweater, very cool light jacket—all good.

The salesman then had me try on a pair of shoes. My hipness quotient is normally quite low, but these were the hippest shoes I had ever seen. They just dripped coolness. I had to have these shoes. I turned the shoe over to check . . . to check, um, where they were made. Yeah, that's it—where they were made. I couldn't help but notice the price. I'm not going to tell you the cost of these shoes; I'll only tell you that I paid less for my first car! (Don't get too excited; it was a 1964 Impala with peeling paint and a bad transmission.)

Talk about discomfort. This was so far outside my paradigm of what a person should pay for shoes that it was ridiculous. But the shoes were perfect for the outfit and the occasion. I found myself in a profound conflict between the perfect shoes and a significant price objection. (Sounds like most of our customers!) Question: Was buying those shoes the right thing for me to do? The salesman decided that it was, and that any other shoe would be unsatisfactory. Here's how the conversation went down:

> ME: "I love the shoes. They really are incredible. I'm just not comfortable paying that much money. It's just too far outside my comfort zone."
>
> SALESMAN: "Okay, you're not comfortable. Fair enough. Let me ask you just one question. Are you comfortable going to this lunch in the shoes you're wearing now?"
> (Pause. Look down. Look up. Pause. Look down. Look up. Pause ...)
>
> ME: "I'll take them."

Let me make it clear that the salesman was not being slick or manipulative. The conversation was natural and comfortable, but there was an appropriate amount of pressure here—pressure that I needed! I was not in a position to make the decision on my own. Otherwise, why would the salesman have needed to be there?

A quick side note: the shoes were made by Allen Edmonds. I am now on my sixth pair of Allen Edmonds shoes, and I have never regretted one purchase.

THE VOICE IN YOUR HEAD (AGAIN)

Remember that there is a constant psychological battle being waged in your head at all times. The motivating force says, "This is a good time to ask them to buy." A competing voice—the comfort addict—says, "Remember what you learned in training: you must earn the right to ask for the sale."

On this point, I am the antitrainer. I am the only sales expert I know of who does not claim to have come up with the saying, "You must earn the right to ask for the sale." I don't know who coined that phrase, but I believe we should deep-six it for good. What a stupid thing to say! (Oh, yes, I am well aware that quite a few people are not going to like me for this one!) I mean, it sounds authoritative and all that, but I believe it is the statement of a comfort addict. Let me explain.

I want to be clear that I do not disagree with the premise that the right to ask for the sale is earned. But I struggle with the idea that we use this as a gut check when we are deep into a buying discussion with a customer. When one voice says, "It's time to ask for the sale," you need not wait to hear another voice say, "You must earn the right." Waiting for that internal exchange will cause you to give up on the closing approximately 100 percent of the time.

Trust the voice! The voice is right. The voice knows what it is doing.

Here is my advice: when the voice in your head suggests that it is time to ask for the sale, *trust the voice!* The voice is right. The voice knows what it is doing. The voice must be heeded.

I would have you think of this another way: by the time the voice says that it's time to ask for the sale, you have already earned the right! Seriously, when was the last time you heard that suggestive voice during the greeting? Never. The voice knows what it is saying, and it knows when it is saying it. Trust the voice.

But let me take this one layer deeper. (I want to see if I can totally blow your mind here.) That voice, the one that tells you to ask for the sale, is not talking to you; it is talking to your customer.

The voice is saying that your customer needs you to ask her to purchase. Does that require boldness on your part? Absolutely, but it is a humble boldness, a servantlike boldness, a boldness that demands that you act in your customer's best interest.

Some people see closing as being disrespectful. I would suggest that the most disrespectful thing you can do is to force your buyer to come back to you, hat in hand, and ask permission to buy your product. Talk about uncomfortable! I would suggest that you have a service-oriented obligation to save your customer from that discomfort.

KATIE AND ROBERT, PART 2

Do you recall from Chapter 4 the story of my daughter and her friend Robert on the family room sofa? Just to reset it for you, I saw that their knees were touching (in violation of house rules!), but I was too uncomfortable to do anything about it. I walked on and made up a story: "They're playing a video game, and they probably don't realize their knees are touching." (Yeah, right.)

Here's the problem: I've been thinking about this boldness stuff for many years, and I knew in real time that I was rationalizing. I caught myself walking through the family room, making up a story, and then literally stopping in my tracks.

"Oh, good grief, Shore. You, sir, are making up a story right here and right now."

Now the plot thickens. You see, if I become aware that I am making up a story, the natural result will be . . . (wait for it) . . . more discomfort! The situation takes on a whole new level of anxiety. My discomfort progression starts all over again. And around we go. . . .

So now I have a whole new Moment of Discomfort, the discomfort of my awareness of my story. And whenever I have a Moment of Discomfort, I also have . . . what? A new Moment of Decision.

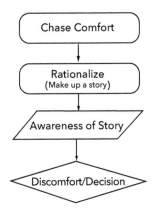

In this case, the choices are clear: Will I confront the situation despite my discomfort, or will I decide that the discomfort is just too great and continue walking? Will I do the bold thing, or will I chase comfort?

Relate that to your sales discomfort for a moment. When we give in to our discomfort during the sales process, we go into storytelling/rationalizing mode. When we become aware that we are telling stories, we now have a new decision to make: Do we continue to chase comfort, or do we make the choice to be bold?

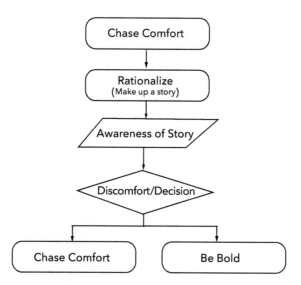

Here's the good news: you still have a choice! At the moment you realize that you are making up a story, there is still time for you to do something bold, to use your discomfort as leverage for action. And that is very good news indeed. This storytelling moment can provide you with an opportunity to change course and to step onto the bold path. But if you choose to continue to chase comfort, the results will be devastating.

Stay with me on this, because by now you realize (if you consult our chart) that it doesn't end there. If I decide to give in to the discomfort, what happens next? Normally, it would be time for a story, right? But I've already used up my story! There is no way to rationalize something that I am already aware of. There is no story left to tell.

There is only one possible outcome at this point: my standards have to go lower.

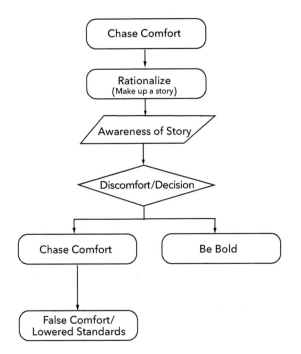

I simply cannot escape this important principle: my standards are not what I desire; they are what I accept. This is true for how I raise my children, for how I run my business, and for how I live my life.

I often hear managers tell me about so-called unacceptable behavior. "The way he talks to people in the finance department is unacceptable." Really? Did you accept it? Because if you accepted it, it's acceptable. Your standards are not what you desire; they are what you accept.

Your standards are not what you desire; they are what you accept.

This is the last, and most tragic, step in the progression of discomfort. There is so much more at stake than just losing a sale. We are dealing with our very own self-paradigm: how we see ourselves and how we define and alter our own moral code.

This addiction to comfort might be more serious than you thought when you first started reading. That's all the more reason to do something about it. It's time to be bold . . . and win the sale!

The Discomfort Progression

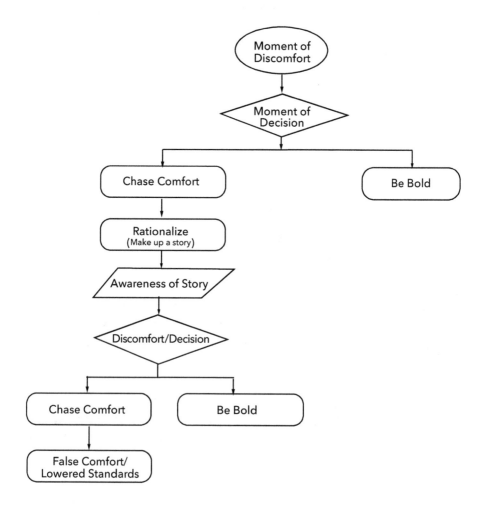

Questions to Ponder

- Has your discomfort ever held you back from helping someone who needed it? How did you rationalize this to yourself in the Moment of Decision? Similarly, have you ever overcome your discomfort and helped someone despite your initial reaction? How did that make you feel afterward?

- Do you connect with the concept of boldly serving your customer's best interests? Can you think of a time that a customer may have settled for less than he or she deserved as a result of your discomfort?

- Consider this statement: my standards are not what I desire; they are what I accept. Have you ever accepted standards that are lower than those you truly desired? Did you acknowledge that you were lowering your standards, or did you find a way to rationalize your choice?

Now Try This . . .

Make a list of 12 standards that you desire to live out in your life. Don't feel constrained; these can include ideas like "Deeply care for my customers," "Earn more this year than last year," "Be actively involved in my children's lives," "Be the number one salesperson on the team," "Give back to my community," "Retire in 10 years," or whatever else true success looks like for you. Take this opportunity to cast a vision for your life that defines what is acceptable to you . . . and, by implication, what is not.

1. _____

2. _____

3. _____

4. _____

5. _____

6. _____

7. _____

8. _____

9. _____

10. _____

11. _____

12. _____

Expert Interview: Linda Richardson

Linda Richardson is one of the most profound thinkers in the sales industry today. I first read her book *Sales Coaching* when I was national sales director for one of the largest home-building firms in the world. Upon finishing the book, I immediately bought copies for all my managers. Linda's book remains a fresh and relevant tool today.

When she is not teaching as an adjunct professor at the Wharton School of Business, Linda runs Richardson Sales Training & Strategy, through which she works with companies around the world. Her latest book, *The New Sales Conversation*, provides a road map for building a sales process in today's entirely new business environment.

Tell me how you first became interested in the study of sales.

I worked for a large bank in New York City at a time when banking was not particularly competitive. Then Citibank came along and changed the norm. In the midst of our company's bleeding clients, my boss called us into an auditorium one day and announced that henceforth, we were all in sales.

I was given the task of selecting a training program, but everything I found was generic. I wanted a program that had a certain attitude to it, but that also included an inherent respect for the client. I needed something specialized, and I couldn't find it, so I created it. I fell in love with sales training right then and there.

Was it a difficult "sell" inside your own company?

It was excruciating. Most of our divisions didn't want anything to do with sales training. Fortunately, I found one struggling division that was *receptive* and ran with it. The results were tremendous, but in the process, I learned something important: developing a sales program wasn't only about the training. The salespeople needed coaching along with education. So, I developed a program for that as well.

Some time later, you wrote the outstanding book *Sales Coaching*. What is it about coaching, in particular, that is a draw for you?

I am a very exact person. I could have written a more overarching book about sales leadership or sales management, but I had seen too many managers take theoretical leadership courses that did not help them apply what they learned. I saw the need for a resource that was much more specific and practical with regard to sales application and coaching.

There is an enormous gap between leadership and the important subset of leadership that we call coaching. I strongly believe that the biggest available gain comes through systematic sales coaching. I knew that as leaders, we could provide great training, but for any organization to truly embrace the lessons taught, those lessons would need to be continually and specifically reinforced through coaching.

I talk a great deal about the need for sales professionals to practice boldness in the face of discomfort. How would you apply that concept to sales leaders?

I think the problem is that many managers find coaching to be subjective. When they show up, they think that they are prepared for a sales coaching encounter, but they don't have a system in mind. That is when they flounder.

I believe that being bold in coaching begins with a specific sales process, something that takes the subjectivity out of it. This allows a manager to focus on something other than personality. Starting out with systematic questions such as, "Did you get feedback from the prospect, or didn't you? Did you share unique value, or didn't you?" is an effective (and objective) way to start.

I find that many managers are uncomfortable with coaching in difficult situations. They dread the idea of giving negative feedback.

Effective sales leaders must have a strong degree of what I call "emotional courage." That courage is developed by moving away from subjectivity and relying on the process, both the sales process and the coaching process.

First, leaders need to know how to coach. It is not as easy as it would seem. There is a science to sales coaching that most managers never learn.

Second, they need to know what to coach to. If there is not a defined and understood sales process in place, the manager will have a difficult time focusing on the right behaviors.

Practice is uncomfortable for most people, especially the dreaded role playing. How do you encourage leaders to overcome their own discomforts in getting their sales teams to spend more time honing their skills?

I greatly value training, but it has to be presented in small bites. Training should include practicing how to practice. This must be a *roll-up-your-sleeves* event, not a boring lecture. There are some key steps in making a practicing-how-to-practice event constructive.

First, establish a safe environment. If you put people on the spot without giving them the chance to practice, you aren't accomplishing anything positive.

Second, get their input. You want to take a collaborative approach to the improvement process. You need to find out how people are thinking, and you must include their individual perspectives and opinions. It's about the questions you ask, not about the PowerPoints you have to share.

Most managers are good at prescribing, but not so strong when it comes to diagnosing. The cardinal rule of sales coaching is: the salesperson talks first!

How would you recommend that a sales leader overcome his or her discomfort when it comes to coaching?

The coaching process should follow the sales process, and that sales process can't be a mystery. There has to be a scientific progression that we can coach to so that we can teach to the process, not the emotion. If we know and rely on the process, it helps us overcome our discomforts because we have a "bigger picture" in mind. Uncomfortable steps along the way to a goal are less painful when one has faith in the ultimate outcome. When sales leaders know the sales process well enough to fully trust in it, that confidence will propel them through uncomfortable coaching moments.

The other half of the equation is to know how to coach. It's not confrontation; it's collaboration. It's not a drubbing; it's a dialogue.

You have a new book out, *The New Sales Conversation*. Tell us about it.

Today's buyers have radically different buying habits from those in the past. With customers relying heavily on the Internet and social media, the salesperson now enters the sales process much later than he or she used to. The understanding of "value" has also changed. Competition in sales is now so great that quality alone doesn't guarantee a sale. The sales professional must have strong expertise in finding and applying solutions for today's prospects. Today's customers are looking for collaboration and creative ideas. This is a far cry from information dumping. My book deals with how to create and shape opportunities in this new sales landscape. We need new models and new techniques.

DEVELOPING BOLDNESS

Our map is now complete—on the discomfort side of the equation. But there is much more to come, and it is one hundred kinds of exciting.

You may be feeling beaten down or depressed or . . . uncomfortable. Good for you! Embrace it! (I'll show you how to do this in Part II.) And if you are feeling crummy, take heart: I promise that the rest of the book is about tested methods for overcoming addictions to comfort and building your boldness muscle. The hard part will be the application of those methods. Might I suggest that you begin with a decision right now to do the bold thing and apply what you learn? Pledge right now to take the steps needed to abandon your own addiction to comfort.

To encourage you, here's a sneak peek at what lies ahead. What if discomfort were a good thing? What if we could reprogram our brains to appreciate, or even embrace, discomfort?

Discomfort during the sales process is normal and natural, and that means that the discomfort you face is faced by sales professionals all over the world. You are neither weird nor broken; you are normal.

We know that different people respond to discomfort in different ways: some by giving in and going down the easy path, and others by tackling the discomfort head-on and reaping the benefits thereafter. These different responses prove that the discomfort itself is not the problem!

Discomfort is neutral and unfeeling. It is not some sort of demon that crouches behind doors, waiting to spring out and attack. Discomfort is like a knife on a counter. On its own, that knife can do nothing but sit there. Depending on how we approach the knife, we can see it as a weapon or as a tool. It is in our response to discomfort that we find the greatest lessons.

Again, what if discomfort were a good thing? What if we could reprogram our brains to appreciate, or even embrace, discomfort? We can, and we will.

6

Let's Do This Thing!
The Remedy

Action is the foundational key to all success.

—PABLO PICASSO

THE BIG IDEA
Boldness is more about action than about attitude.

Let me share a very interesting (and admittedly troubling) case study that was brought to me by a sales professional who sells homes in Austin, Texas. As she was showing a home to a couple, the husband and wife had dramatically different responses. The wife loved the home and communicated this fact emotionally and enthusiastically. Her husband was as cold as ice throughout the entire process and looked as if he would gladly have been anywhere else on the planet but in that home. The couple left without making a purchase decision.

The very next day, the wife returned without her husband to see the home a second time. Once again her emotions came through; to her, the home was perfect in every way. When the sales counselor inquired about her husband's lack of enthusiasm for the home, the wife's response was vague, at best.

What would you do? Do you have a sense that the salesperson was missing something here? Customers often have deep feelings associated with the buying process, emotions that they are not in any hurry to divulge. Why is this? Well, there could be many reasons for a customer to be guarded, not the least of which is that the customer may fear that sharing more than the most minimally necessary information could leave him vulnerable to an unscrupulous salesperson. Or perhaps it's for the simple reason that telling someone you don't know very well all the ins and outs of why you are shopping in the first place is just not comfortable. Whatever the reason behind a customer's being guarded, it always boils down to the same thing: that ever-present discomfort.

At some point, it is the job of the bold sales professional to ask the deeper and more difficult questions in order to get an accurate picture of what is happening in a customer's life. That kind of inquiry might go something like this:

> "Look, there is clearly something about this situation that I do not fully understand. I want to help, but I cannot truly serve your needs unless I know what is really happening here. Talk to me. Tell me what I don't know."

Clearly, this is a bold approach. Asking questions like this requires a strong belief that you serve your customers most effectively when you know their situation most thoroughly. Asking deeper questions like this may not be comfortable, but it is the right thing to do. We must not let our own desire for comfort make us watered-down versions of ourselves, too afraid to "go there" with someone who is clearly holding something back.

The mindset of top performers is that they are providing a valuable service to their customers by asking the deeper questions. They don't see this as a personal affront in any way; they are simply doing their jobs as trusted advisors to their clients.

Back to our scenario. The new home salesperson asked her prospect just such a deep and important question. The customer paused for a moment before letting out a deep sigh, a form of nonverbal communication that essentially says, "I give up. I cannot keep this inside any longer." Then she divulged the following:

> "Our . . . our teenage son was killed by a drunk driver about six months ago. I don't know what to tell you, except that I feel like I am living in my own haunted house. Every corner I turn is another painful moment. I have to move. My husband sees this in a completely different way. To him, our home is a shrine to our son, the place where his memory can live on. He cannot begin to understand how I can even think about leaving it right now."

I'm going to assume that you are reading this story from the perspective of the salesperson, and I'll ask you to let this story sink in for a moment. I think it is safe to say that we wouldn't want to be in that salesperson's shoes.

> *Dig deep to find the courage to ask the really important questions.*

Or would we? The fact is that this couple is going through a traumatic version of hell on earth, whether the salesperson knows it or not. And the decisions they will make are dictated by their circumstances, whether the salesperson knows about those circumstances or not. In other words, I'm not sure that "dumb and happy" is really the best place to be in this case.

I want to encourage you to dig deep to find the courage to ask the really important questions. Your desire for comfort will naturally advise you to hit the brakes when the answers start to get sensitive and awkward. You must fight this instinct.

BE THE DOCTOR

Consider my physician. As a middle-aged male, I have to tell you that my physicals have come to involve a certain uncomfortable element. (Oh, please tell me that I do not need to elaborate on my explanation of where this is going!) During my last examination, we got to the point where my doctor was donning a latex glove.

"Oh, great, the fun part," I said glumly.

He replied, "If it makes you feel better, this is not exactly the highlight of my day."

I chuckled at that, but I was also hit with a realization: that statement did, in fact, make me feel better. If this *was* the highlight of his day, we would have had a problem!

A short time later, I was driving back home (softly weeping over the experience) when something occurred to me. There had to have been a first time that this doctor had had to perform that procedure. It was probably in medical school, and in all probability the procedure was performed on another medical student.

Question: The first time he performed the procedure, who was more uncomfortable, the doctor or the patient? I would contend that the doctor experienced far greater discomfort.

Now suppose the doctor carried over that discomfort into his practice. We would get to this point in the examination, and his discomfort would arise in a big way. His internal mental monologue might sound something like this:

Oh, man ... I hate this. I mean I hate this! Mom said, "The world needs podiatrists," but noooo, I had to study general medicine. I don't want to do this, and I know Mr. Shore doesn't want me to do this, either. And really, he's a healthy guy. His weight is good; he eats right; his blood pressure is in check. I mean, what are the odds that he has prostate cancer? Pretty low! Will it really hurt anything if we skip this part of the physical?

Would he feel better if he eliminated that step in the examination? In the short run, yes. Would I feel better if he eliminated it? Dang straight, I would ... for a while. In the long run, we would both know that my best interests had not been served.

At the end of the day, I want to know that my service provider is acting in my best interests, and that means overcoming discomfort on his or her part. (And next time you feel uncomfortable asking a prospect a question about unspoken issues, just remember this story and be glad that your vocation does not require sanitized latex gloves.)

THE REMEDY

By now you are aware that the remedy comes down to one word: boldness. And if you are like me, your first response to this may be something like, "Duh." It seems both obvious and dramatically oversimplified if we stop there, so let's start by making sure we agree on the definition.

Stop for a moment and ask yourself the question, "What is boldness?" Chew on that and really give it some consideration. It is important that you are clear on the concept in your own mind. Take a moment and write down your own definition in the following space.

My definition of boldness is . . .

_____

_____

_____

_____

Now that you have your from-the-gut definition in place, let's explore what others have said. I'll begin with Webster's dictionary, which offers this technical definition:

Fearless before danger; showing or requiring a fearless, daring spirit.

I must take exception to one part of this definition: the implication that there is no room for fear in the definition of boldness. This suggestion of fear-lessness appears in definitions from various sources. I disagree. One can be fearful *and* bold at the same time.

Here are several definitions I received in response to a query asking sales-people to offer a definition of boldness without looking anything up.

- "The courage to go beyond and push further than you think you're even capable of."
- "The ability to be the best version of your true self, without regret."
- "A determination to act to achieve the best possible outcome without fear or doubt."
- "Moving forward with conviction in the face of everyone else retreating."
- "The courage to do what others won't."
- "Stepping up when others are frozen in fear."
- "Being consciously aggressive in what you believe to be correct."
- "Taking a chance and doing something you believe is right, no matter what the outcome."
- "Having enough confidence to take action in the moment."
- "The willingness to act on, speak about, or address something you are passionate about, even if it is out of your comfort zone."
- "Jumping right in front of what may be fearful and saying 'Bring it on!'"

I hope you see what I saw in those responses: the very thought of boldness seems to stir a passion in people, especially salespeople. They believe that boldness is a good and a beneficial thing, even though many of them acknowledge that boldness can come at a cost.

CHARACTERISTIC OR SKILL SET?

As we home in on a helpful definition, I would like to investigate one more thing: Is boldness a skill or a characteristic? Is it based on nature or nurture? Is it something we are born with or something that we develop over time?

Again, dwell on that for a moment. While you're thinking, I'm going to make the question easier for you to handle by eliminating one possible answer: "both." For this mental exercise, I want you to decide on one or the other. So if, for example, you are thinking that boldness is 51 percent nature and 49 percent nurture, your answer is nature. Take a moment and come up with your answer now.

It is quite possible that you have been taught that boldness falls into the category of "personality trait." A salesperson can be labeled bold, just as he or she can be described as good-natured, pessimistic, outgoing, or ornery. To answer the question, let me ask another: Can boldness be learned and developed? If you think not, and are not willing to reconsider, you can set this book down right now; I have nothing left to say. I contend that boldness, especially sales boldness, can *and must* be learned.

If boldness can be taught, then it must be a skill set, not a characteristic. Boldness can be learned and developed. There is no physiological reason why you cannot be bold in your own way. Boldness is a skill set ... so let's get to work!

BOLDNESS: A DEFINITION

Allow me to offer the following definition of boldness. It will serve as a centering point for our further discussions:

> *Boldness is taking action to do the right thing, despite the fear and the discomfort.*

Note a very important aspect of this definition: boldness is defined as an *action* rather than an *attitude*. It is based not upon how you feel, but upon what you do. While the proper attitude is critical, it is action that defines boldness.

Think back on your own bold moves: standing firm when you were faced with a tough objection, asking for the sale when you were afraid to do so, or asking for it a second (or third) time. In every case, it was the action that was bold. While the attitude must be there, the action deserves the glory. Embracing risk is an action. Appreciating change is an action. Doing the tough thing is an action. I'm guessing that you are already bolder than you have realized. We get so used to certain kinds of necessary boldness in our lives that we become blind to them and start to think that we do not have the capacity for increased (or, worse yet, *any*) boldness. We do. *You* do.

> *Boldness is defined as an action rather than an attitude.*

NECESSARY BOLDNESS

One way we know that boldness is an action rather than an attitude is to simply look at those times when boldness is necessitated by circumstance.

When Emily, my oldest daughter, was just four years old, we went to the Children's Discovery Museum in San Jose, California, for a family outing. It was a pleasant day that was made more memorable than it should have been for one reason: I lost track of Emily. At four years old, she blended in all too well with the veritable swarm of tiny people; what started out as calm concern quickly escalated to a frantic search. I called out for Emily, first in subdued tones, but as more time went by, my calls became loud and urgent. I am not normally one to approach strangers in a crowd, but in this case, I found myself asking anyone and everyone if they had seen a little girl who looked lost. By now I was frantically shouting for her, and several people had joined me in the search.

I practically cried when Emily came around a corner; my wife had found her wandering around with a look of concern on her face, worried that she had been abandoned.

All ended well in that story, but think about what those circumstances inspired me to do. I yelled loudly in a confined space. I approached complete strangers, begging for their assistance. I set every bit of dignity aside in order to communicate the gravity of the situation. And why? Because of the urgency of the moment. Boldness was not an option; it was an absolute necessity.

> *Boldness will appear when the motivation is strong enough.*

When the will is strong enough, the action follows. In that situation, the boldness appeared with the motivation. Let me repeat that . . . *the boldness appeared with the motivation.* It's gut-check time, my friends. It is time to ask yourself how badly you want it. Do you really have the desire to be the best you can be? The boldness will appear when the motivation is strong enough.

THE PARADOX OF "HUMBLE BOLDNESS"

Think back to our definition: "Boldness is taking action to do the right thing, despite the fear and the discomfort." We began by determining that "taking action" was a necessary part of the definition, and now we move on to another important aspect: doing the "right thing."

Some people might see boldness as a license to bully. Boldness can be viewed as taking an opportunity to be self-centered and manipulative, with an "I'm getting mine" approach. To be sure, there is a potentially ugly side to boldness. Saddam Hussein was bold. Hitler was bold. Money-centered televangelists are bold. Sleazy salespeople are bold.

That kind of boldness is not what I'm talking about. In fact, I would be horrified if anyone reading this book took my message in that way. When I talk about boldness, I have in mind a "humble boldness" that is largely opposite from the type of boldness that tyrants and sleazeballs employ. Humble boldness means that I act in the interest of my customers, not myself. Humble boldness is about serving. It means that I consider how my own goals and dreams affect the people I am selling to. It means that there is a time to take a stand, and also a time to (boldly) remain silent.

THE ULTIMATE EXAMPLE

The best possible picture of humble boldness that I know of is found in the life of Jesus Christ. If you are looking for the ultimate example of someone who gave no thought to his own comfort, look no further.

Here are just a few examples of humble boldness in the life of Jesus:

- Jesus healed a leper by . . . touching him! Such an action was seriously taboo. Let's face it: it is extremely uncomfortable to care about those we find to be "unlovable."

- Jesus hung out with the undesirables of society. The religious establishment mocked him for this, but his mission was more important to him than pleasing the authorities.

- Jesus denounced religious traditions that were done not out of conviction of the heart, but only out of obligation and for the sake of appearance.

- Even Jesus' own family rejected him. Talk about uncomfortable!

I could go on, of course; this is a topic I am passionate about. I'll leave it at this: you were created for more than your own comfort. Jesus' entire life provides a beautiful illustration of what this means. The world needs no more selfishness than it already has. Be bold . . . and serve!

Questions to Ponder

- Have you ever sold to a customer who held back unspoken issues? How did you uncover those issues? How did the information change your approach to serving that customer's best interests?

- Think back to the first time you ever talked to a customer in a sales environment. Who was more uncomfortable—you or the customer? What did you learn about yourself by persevering through that discomfort? Did your level of discomfort change as you gained new positive experiences?

- Do you find yourself defining boldness differently today from the way you defined it yesterday? How does the idea of "action more than attitude" affect your perception of boldness? Where can you apply more action in your sales efforts right now?

Now Try This . . .

Take a moment to write down three bold accomplishments that you would like to achieve during the coming months. These can be specific sales accomplishments, or they can also include other life aspirations:

1. _____

2. _____

3. _____

Now it's time to examine the link between your attitudes, your actions, and your accomplishments.

1. Using the table below, write down those three bold accomplishments in the cells titled "Bold Accomplishment."

2. Define and write down a bold (but humble) attitude that motivates you toward each of the bold accomplishments.

3. Write down one specific bold action that you can take right now to build a bridge between your attitude and your accomplishments.

4. *Take action today!*

Bold Accomplishment	Bold (but Humble) Attitude	Bold Action

Expert Interview: Larry Winget

If you've never experienced Larry Winget before, I would encourage you to go to his website (larrywinget.com) and view his videos. Before you do that, prepare yourself—I can promise that absolutely no punches will be pulled.

Larry is the "Pitbull of Personal Development," and the label fits extremely well. With a series of *New York Times* bestselling books with titles including *People Are Idiots and I Can Prove It!* and *Shut Up, Stop Whining, and Get a Life*, Larry provides hard-hitting instruction that gets to the core of living a bold life.

Larry Winget is a tell-it-like-it-is kind of guy who is not a slave to potential discomfort. Perhaps the very best way to describe Larry is, "He gets letters."

In your study of self-limiting behavior, what is the number one thing that holds people back from their own success?

That's an easy answer for me. It's what I consider to be the biggest problem not just for people, but for all of society: being crippled by a sense of entitlement. People forget that you have to work to get results, and that means doing the tough things. The only thing we are "entitled" to is the opportunity to achieve and do well.

This dynamic feeds itself throughout society. Schools award a trophy for just showing up, not for achievement. But that's not the way the world works.

The sales world has the same problem. Salespeople who are raised in an environment of entitlement expect everyone to say yes. It's harder to get started in sales today because new salespeople are not used to rejection.

It's interesting that my own message doesn't resonate with the young the way it does with those who are more world-savvy. I offer one guarantee of success: you're going to fail all along the way. That's obvious in selling, or at least it should be. You're going to get a whole lot of noes before you get a yes.

Do you think boldness is more of an inherited characteristic or a learned state, and why?

Interesting question. I'm working on a new book called *Grow a Pair*. I teach people to take back their lives through a series of bold actions. Yes, I believe boldness can be taught and nurtured.

But this is not a technique; it's a way of thinking differently. The technique-driven salesperson says, "Give me a good enough line and I'll make the sale." That's not the answer. We need to teach the principles of boldness, not a reinvented sales technique.

I think it's safe to say that you have a very bold approach. Did that come naturally to you, or have you become bolder over the years?

It wasn't natural at all. It was a series of little steps right from the start. I used to struggle with really difficult lines like, "Hello, my name is Larry Winget."

I had to learn to play the game. I started playing the business game, which meant, I thought, making other people happy. I played the game with the idea that I was in the world to please others.

I used to speak to make people happy. I spoke for the smiles and the applause and the laughter and the standing ovation. But I wasn't giving my speech. In time, I had a crisis—I hated my audience, my business model, even myself. It was inauthentic. There was a bold person with a bold message, but I was stifling that.

I made a bold decision. I was willing to throw away the suits, put the earrings back in, and say what I really wanted to say. I discovered that people don't really listen to what you have to say, or even believe it, but they always listen to see if you believe what you have to say.

When people listen to me, they don't have to agree with me (and, yes, I get letters!). But they really admire the fact that I say what needs to be said.

If you were giving the commencement address at a high school today, what would your top piece of advice be?

Interesting that you should ask. I recently appeared on Fox News to provide something of a commencement address. [Author's note: I watched this video on Larry's website. Wish I'd seen it 25 years ago!]

The first step is that you have to take responsibility for your own success. You can't wait for anyone to hand you your life on a platter. Second, be respectful to the people around you, and to the company you work for. Even if your boss is an idiot, he is still your boss. Third, establish clear priorities. Your time, energy, and money will always go to what is important to you. And finally, work hard and give it your best effort. It's not about passion or happiness in the workplace; it's about hard work and excellent results.

What do you say to those who have what I call "comfort addictions"?

In my line of work, I want to make people uncomfortable in order to make them think for themselves. When they think for themselves and understand the benefits of dealing with their discomfort, they are required to make a decision. How they respond will make all the difference in their lives.

The Boldness Workout
Strengthening the "Boldness Muscle"

Endure and persist; this pain will turn to good by and by.

—Ovid

THE BIG IDEA
To build boldness, you must choose your response before a decision is thrust upon you.

I have had to come to grips with an unpleasant reality over the last several years: I'm not as young as I once was, and my body can no longer perform the superhuman feats that I imagine it once did.

A few years back, I was invited to take part in a pickup soccer scrimmage, a "friendly" event at a local high school on a Saturday morning. What I was not told was that this game was putting up a bunch of hacks like me against the varsity soccer team from that local high school as a way for the very talented young men to practice their skills under game conditions.

I realized that I was in over my head long before I stepped onto "the pitch," but hey—I worked out fairly regularly, and that included aerobic exercise; how bad could it be? (Don't answer.)

Remarkably and inexplicably, I scored a goal in the first few minutes of the game. I would describe that moment to you in all its glory, except that I never actually saw it take place. I was standing in a group in front of the goal when the ball suddenly shot out of nowhere, struck me in the back, and careened into the net. I felt something hit me, and the next thing I knew, people around me were offering congratulations. This was going better than I had anticipated!

I should have faked an injury and walked off the field right then and there, but my newly puffed-up ego commanded me to stay put. Less than a minute later, I was back on defense when the ball was kicked a mile into the air from the other side of the field, right at me. I saw it descending from on high, growing larger as it lost altitude. I thought to myself, "I've watched soccer games on television, and I know what happens next. My job is to head this ball in the opposite direction from whence it came. How hard can that be?"

Bad idea. I thrust my ample forehead in the direction of the ball and sent it launching back up the field. I would continue with the rest of the story, but that is about all I can remember. The moment was cartoonlike, complete with tweeting birds and stars circling my head. Someone complimented me on the excellent strike, but quickly followed up with, "You OK?"

I stayed in the game for a time (pride is a powerful, yet stupid motivator), but I was clearly proving to be even less useful than I had been up to that point. Eventually, I just walked off the field and wished the team good luck.

The next morning, I could barely get up. My legs felt as if a Buick had parked on them all night. My head was throbbing, and I could feel every pulse. I asked my wife to get me four hundred aspirin.

I haven't played soccer since.

You have some sort of similar story, I would guess—a time when your brain convinced you that you could do more than your body could handle . . . and you paid the price. The older I get, the more I realize my own limitations. (Insert exasperated sigh here.)

My mother taught me many things in her incredible life, including an unwavering loyalty to the San Francisco 49ers. I had the great pleasure of watching some of the best football players ever to step onto the gridiron: Joe

Montana, Ronnie Lott, Dwight Clark, and the greatest wide receiver ever to play the game, Jerry Rice.

Rice was not the fastest receiver in the league, or the tallest, or the most athletic, yet his list of accomplishments reads as every young boy's wish list. He is the NFL's all-time record-holder in receptions, yards, and touchdowns. He won three Super Bowls and was named Most Valuable Player in Super Bowl XXIII. He holds nearly every possible receiving record for both regular season and postseason play. In 2010, the year he was inducted into the Hall of Fame, the NFL Network honored Rice as the greatest player in the history of the game.

Jerry Rice played professional football for 20 years, an almost unheard of tenure for an NFL player. The secret to his longevity: The Hill.

The Hill is a 2.5-mile incline at the Edgewood Park and Nature Preserve in Redwood City, California, a short drive south from San Francisco. Making it to the top is an accomplishment; running to the top is inhuman. It is a trail where many an athlete has fallen to his knees and regretted eating that hearty breakfast. Jerry Rice ran The Hill every day as part of his rigorous workout regimen. Says Rice of The Hill: "Leave your ego at the bottom."

Rice was renowned for his work ethic. His grueling routines, both on- and off-season, were legendary. Somewhere behind the fame, the glory, the records, and the accolades there is a foundation of very hard work. Most quit at the moment of discomfort. The best of the best plow forward despite the pain, motivated by a palpable desire to win.

> *Nothing stops the man who desires to achieve. Every obstacle is simply a course to develop his achievement muscle. It's a strengthening of his powers of accomplishment.*
> —THOMAS CARLYLE

Building your boldness muscle is all about commitment and dedication. Novice bike riders feel a tremendous burn on a relatively slight slope; experienced riders can climb mountains. Beginning weight lifters feel tremendous pain after their first workouts, while advanced resistance trainers have to push hard to feel that same burn. Likewise, boldness is a muscle group. The good news is that, as with any muscle group, boldness can be grown. We can increase our boldness strength with regular use and continual stressing. In fact, boldness *must* be developed if we are to reach our true potential.

The converse is also true. Muscular atrophy is described as a wearing away of muscle mass through prolonged rest. This can be caused by disease, but it can also occur through lack of use. I broke a bone in my hand as a teenager and had to have a cast up to my elbow in order for it to heal. The unused muscles weakened, as my hand was completely immobilized for quite some time. Atrophy set in during the recovery period, and when the cast was removed and I was ready to start using my hand again, I couldn't. This is the problem with muscular atrophy: when you really *need* the muscle, it just isn't available. It's not strong enough to do the job you want and need it to do. So, too, with boldness. If we give in to our desire for comfort long enough, then even when we need and want to be bold, we lack the mental muscle power to do so.

NO PAIN, NO GAIN

By now you probably understand that part of the process I am prescribing calls for embracing discomfort. If you've ever followed a physical exercise regimen, you know that discomfort is a normal and expected part of a workout. You know that working out will not be comfortable, but you also know that the real gains occur when you push through the pain and go for the extra rep, add the extra weight, or run the extra mile.

I would be modestly uncomfortable if I were to pick up 5 pounds in each hand and do 20 curls. I would be mighty uncomfortable if I picked up 30 pounds in each hand and attempted to do 12 curls. The question is, which would give me greater results?

As you train your boldness muscles, keep in mind that what you will get out of your "workout" depends on what you are willing to put into it. I'm not suggesting that you put yourself in the position of trying to tackle your gnarliest discomfort in life right off the bat, just as I would not suggest that you begin a workout routine by running 10 miles on day one. We all know that big goals are achieved by taking many small steps to reach them. But resist the temptation to choose *comfortable* small steps. Just as in a physical workout, even small changes will produce big results in building boldness within you if you *continually* and *consistently* challenge yourself. Even a small pain leads to gain.

That said, in the long run, you should be thinking big. You should be planning ahead for that major boldness opportunity that you have already identified. It has often been said that "excuses will always be there for you; opportunity won't." While that is absolutely true, do not let the risk of failure if you attempt to reach for that opportunity prevent you from working hard and risking failure. The sooner you reach the point of failure, the sooner the strengthening will begin. Maintaining mediocrity is easy. Building boldness requires a willingness to push past failure.

DEVELOPING THE FAST-TWITCH "BOLDNESS MUSCLE"

When we talk about our physical muscles, we are generally referring to those that are attached to our bones. We tend to subconsciously assume the truth of the simple equation of muscle = strength. End of story. But not all muscle tissue is alike. As it relates to athletic performance, there are two different types of muscle groups. Generically, these are described as "slow-twitch" and "fast-twitch" muscles. Slow-twitch muscles provide steady support for a long period of time, while fast-twitch muscles are powerful in short bursts.

Fast- and slow-twitch muscles are the perfect reflection of our mental muscles. Our mental slow-twitch muscles are what we have just discussed—those that we add gradual strength to over time, making us stronger and stronger until we can do really impressive things. When we have strengthened our slow-twitch mental muscles, we are able to handle the major discomforts of life, systematically working toward dismantling our stories and building confidence as we move toward humble boldness.

But what about everyday (fast-twitch) discomforts? It's one thing to look at superhuman endeavors or major life projects. What about the small, seemingly insignificant uncomfortable moments that we endure each day? How do we respond to a snide remark, a spur-of-the-moment procrastination, or the objection that we did not see coming?

> *We must retrain our minds to respond positively and automatically to these moments—to consistently choose a more positive result. And in order to retrain, we must first untrain.*

We must retrain our minds to respond positively and automatically to these moments—to consistently choose a more positive result. And in order to retrain, we must first *untrain*. We must come to grips with the stories and rationalizations that are part of our everyday lives. As we continue on our journey, we will retrain our brains just as athletes train their bodies.

Athletes train so that their muscles respond automatically to the task at hand when they need them to. Their fast-twitch muscles fire seemingly of their own will with bursts of power and quickness. Think of a running back who suddenly spots a small gap in the offensive line 12 inches to the left of where he is running. He must turn to make a sharp cut to the left while his momentum is carrying him forward. He plants his right leg and explodes to the left, leaving the would-be tackler grasping at air.

> *Our fast-twitch mental muscles must be trained to take over when discomfort rears its ugly head.*

In the same way, our fast-twitch mental muscles must be trained to take over when discomfort rears its ugly head. These mental muscles can and must overpower the stories that pop up, replacing them with predetermined positive actions in favor of boldness.

THE DECISION *BEFORE* THE DECISION

My wife and I took swing dance lessons in preparation for our son's wedding because we wanted to dance without looking foolish. (OK, *I* wanted to dance without looking foolish.) Learning to dance was uncomfortable and often frustrating, but we eventually got to the point where we could pull off a few moves.

After we had learned the basics of the East Coast Swing, we still had to actually dance . . . in front of people! We didn't think it would be wise to make our "debut" at the wedding reception, so we decided to go to a club and give it a shot. I confess that this was a radically uncomfortable decision. The very idea of dancing in front of people—even strangers—was incredibly stressful to me, so I was not sure how I would respond when I actually got to the club.

The key for us was to make a positive decision *before* we faced our moment of discomfort. In sales and in life, most of the familiar moments of discomfort can be predicted with some degree of accuracy. If they can be predicted, then we can predetermine our response. In other words, I can train my mental muscles *before* I need to use them. I cannot emphasize this strongly enough. Training your fast-twitch mental muscles is about the work that you do *in the gym*, not on the playing field.

We had to make our decision to dance in advance. Were we to make the decision during our moment of discomfort (at the club), we would tap into a lower plane in our brain—that emotion-driven comfortable place. I knew for a fact that my emotional brain would say, "Run away!" However, when we made the decision to dance *in advance*, without the emotion associated with the moment of discomfort, we were able to choose that action through a higher center of the brain, our ethical plane. The right thing to do was to dance.

When we arrived at the club, we noticed that the live band was rocking and the club-goers were . . . sitting in chairs around the dance floor looking as if they were waiting their turn for an IRS audit. My wife and I had to remind ourselves of our premade decision. Dancing in front of people was one thing; doing so when no one else was dancing seemed like quite another. That would make us the center of the show . . . that was a whole new level of discomfort! Had we not already made the decision to dance, we would have joined the crowd and had a seat, but we had made the decision . . . and so we danced.

Was it uncomfortable to dance on an open floor with complete strangers observing and evaluating? (At least, that's the story I told myself: that strangers cared about my dance moves.) Yep, it was mighty uncomfortable. But it wasn't two minutes before another couple got up . . . and another . . . and another. The band's attitude picked up. The energy grew. Soon people were dancing, smiling, and singing along as they left their inhibitions behind.

This is one of the amazing things about making predecisions to be bold: doing so gives you an inherent *freedom*. My wife and I *did* feel uncomfortable about starting to dance, but it was a short-lived discomfort because we had already made the decision before we were in the moment. Because of that decision, *we were freed up to take action*. There was nothing to discuss with each other, and our feelings of discomfort did not last that long because our predecision made the process simple. We were going to dance, no matter what. We were freed from ourselves (and each other) by having a plan and sticking to it. And, somewhat surprisingly, our bold action freed up those around us.

I encourage you to make bold decisions *now*. Determine your future success *right now*! Go into boldness training immediately. Don't wait for your discomfort to dictate your level of success.

BOLDNESS FROM AN ETHICAL PERSPECTIVE

My statement that our decision to dance was made not from the lower emotional part of our brains, but from the upper ethical portion might have you wondering how dancing is a matter of ethics. In its simplest vernacular meaning, *ethics* is a set of moral principles; it is about doing the right thing. Staying with that simple definition, was dancing the right thing to do? Would it have been wrong for us to sit on the sidelines? For me, the answer to both questions is yes.

Our ethical compass tells us what is right and wrong on many levels. It is not just a matter of returning the money when the clerk gives us too much change, or deciding against spreading malicious gossip. This is not about whether someone was wronged in a decision. Ethics is not just about doing the *right* thing; it is also about doing the *best* thing.

> Ethics is not just about doing the right thing; it is also about doing the best thing.

I say this in hopes of further dismantling your default storytelling mentality. We face discomfort, we make up a story, and we move on with our lives. But somewhere during that process, there is a muffled voice in our heads that wants to scream out, "That's wrong!" That voice is our ethical center trying to teach us a better way to live.

Is there more at stake in this concept than making more sales, overcoming difficult objections, or dealing with prospecting fears? I believe there is. I believe that our sense of self is at risk when we continually chase the easy path. I believe that we stifle our potential. Going back to our original definition of ethics, that is just plain wrong.

THE BOLDNESS WORKOUT

By now you've had plenty of time to think through your own tendencies in dealing with sales discomfort, and hopefully you've had the opportunity to discuss those concerns with others. You might even have some specific goals for where you want to go next, for what mountain you want to conquer. It is time to put those thoughts and ideas to work.

I have suggested that a big part of the problem with being bold lies in our immediate, knee-jerk reactions to discomfort. The fast-twitch mental muscles have long been established in each of us, because coming up with a story at the moment of discomfort requires that exact aptitude. It is not a matter of whether or not we have fast-twitch mental muscles (we all do!), but rather a question of whether or not we are using them for our benefit.

Moreover, it is the timing of our decisions that makes all the difference. If we wait until a sales discomfort is staring us in the face before we decide how to deal with it, we will surely fast-twitch our way into yielding to discomfort.

The trick, then, is to get in *front* of the discomfort. You need to decide your response *before* a moment of decision is thrust upon you. This involves an understanding of how your brain works, so let's rely on the experts and take a dive into the world of cognitive behavioral theory. Trust me—the topic is 100 percent fascinating.

> *Training your fast-twitch mental muscles is about the work that you do in the gym, not on the playing field.*

Questions to Ponder

- Have you ever experienced muscular atrophy, physically or metaphorically? How did you regain your muscle strength? How long did the recovery process take? How can you apply this concept to building boldness muscles?

- Why is it important to develop a fast-twitch response to discomfort? How does a rapid response better enable you to respond when you are faced with a Moment of Discomfort? Why are you better equipped when you have chosen your decision in advance of the discomfort?

Now Try This . . .

Take a moment to write down three discomforts that you regularly face. Choose at least one sales discomfort, but feel free to include other general life discomforts.

Think carefully about these discomforts; they will become the foundation for your work in the following chapters:

1. _____

2. _____

3. _____

Next, enter those discomforts in the table below. Then take the time to identify a decision that you can make in advance of each discomfort. Be sure that your decisions are:

- Rooted in an attitude of humble boldness

- Action-oriented

- Consistent with your highest standards

Discomfort	Decision

Expert Interview: Alex Taba

I sold homes for many years, and I always felt that I was selling a very cool product. But Alex Taba sets the bar for cool sales. Alex sells Ferraris and Maseratis, and he is dang good at it!

Alex Taba began his car sales career in the big leagues, selling Porsches. He was salesperson of the month in his very first month on the job, and he has never looked back. Over the past 20-plus years, he has sold nothing but luxury automobiles (Bentleys, Rolls-Royces, Ferraris, Maseratis, and the like) to well-heeled and discriminating buyers. Today you can find him at Penske Automotive at the Wynn Hotel in Las Vegas (one of the coolest showrooms you will ever visit in your lifetime, by the way).

Alex, you sell a high-end product to high-end customers, and you've been successful for your entire career. What accounts for that success?

I am in the perfect line of work for me because I love people and I love cars. This job allows me to match up those passions. I've always been a top producer because I have always been extremely passionate about what I do.

You were salesperson of the month right out of the gate. To what do you attribute that early success?

I'll never forget a manager pulling me aside and saying, "Alex, you were number one because you didn't qualify customers, and therefore you didn't disqualify them either. Don't ever change." That made sense to me. I believe that everyone who comes through my door is there to purchase.

In sales, you have to start with the end result in mind. You have to believe in what will happen in every sales conversation. I envision my customer driving away in a car, and then I just connect the dots to get him there.

It starts with treating people as if they were my own relatives. I'm not going to treat my sister or my cousin in a sleazy, unethical manner. I am going to show her how she can really enjoy the purchasing experience as well as the car.

Because you sell luxury automobiles, you have to deal with the discomfort of price objections. Tell me about how you approach that.

Pricewise, I am selling homes on wheels, so I have to be confident and comfortable about that. If I display discomfort, if I look like I am apologizing for the price of the car, the customer will sense that immediately.

Any discomfort is my own undoing. Clients are always going to be challenging. My job is to make sure that discomfort doesn't take root.

I imagine that you are dealing with a segment of the buying population that can be extremely discriminating. What do you do with the discomfort of dealing with finicky people?

I've sold cars to billionaires, and that is an interesting experience. I think the biggest difference in such people is that they size you up more quickly than anyone else. But the basic principles of human behavior are still in place. People buy from salespeople they like. Conversely, we sell most effectively to customers that we like. If it's not a good relational match, I simply hand the customer over to a peer. Not everyone is going to fall in love with his or her salesperson, and not every salesperson is going to love every customer.

You sell a product that is extremely technologically advanced. How much of your sales process is emotional and how much is technical?

In general, 90 percent is emotional and 10 percent is technical. Some clients have a greater desire to understand the technical aspects, but really, it's an emotional purchase.

I recently sold a car to a woman. That doesn't sound like a big deal, but Ferrari is more typically a male-dominated brand. She was very uncomfortable when it came to some of the key issues of owning a Ferrari: drivability, functionality, upkeep, complexity.

All of these issues were stumbling blocks for her. So what did I sell her on? Luxury, comfort, ease of ownership, beauty—everything she really wanted to buy. You don't have to have a background in racing to want a Ferrari. She was a visual person, and the car is visually amazing. It was perfect for her.

What advice would you offer for someone who is new to sales?

Be passionate and be yourself. If being yourself doesn't work in sales, go do something else. If you're not passionate, again, go do something else. If you have to be someone that you are not in order to do your job, you are going to fail.

Sales is not about being an actor; it's about being genuine. How would you sell to a relative or to your best friend? Treat people that way and you'll figure everything else out.

Retraining Your Brain
Building Bold Thought Patterns

The world turns on our every action, and our every omission, whether we know it or not.

—ABRAHAM VERGHESE, *CUTTING FOR STONE*

THE BIG IDEA
Boldness begins with your thought patterns.
It grows stronger through small decisions and
actions over time.

So far, we have looked at small, quick-strike methods for dealing with common sales discomforts. Now it's time to explore a deeper understanding of those remedies. I will approach this exploration on two different levels in the chapters that follow, beginning with an explanation of the psychological underpinnings of the remedies, using an important and effective psychological approach to discomfort: cognitive behavioral therapy. I believe you will find this quite interesting (I promise to keep it simple), and it will also give you a deeper understanding of the motivations behind the techniques that will follow.

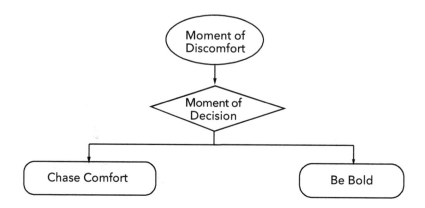

COGNITIVE BEHAVIORAL THERAPY: A PRIMER

To begin with, I will acknowledge the fact that critics often assail the use of proven psychological methods by nonpsychologists. Fine. I readily admit that I am not a psychotherapist, nor do I claim to be an expert in the area of behavioral conditioning. I am a dedicated student (and at times a floundering pilgrim) on this journey, and I have been greatly affected by the principles that follow. Through my own research, I am convinced that when we understand how the brain responds to discomfort, we can more clearly prepare for the common and ordinary discomforts that occur throughout the sales process. So, yes, it's true, I'm not a psychotherapist. (But I play one on TV!)

I'll start with a definition in order to break down the two key components of cognitive behavioral therapy (CBT).

Cognition = thoughts

Behavior = actions

Cognitive behavioral therapy is about training yourself to put your thoughts ahead of your actions.

CBT is about training yourself to put your thoughts ahead of your actions (I told you I'd keep it simple), and about purposefully and intentionally anticipating discomfort in order to make a *decision* (a cognitive act) on how you will *respond* (a behavioral act). The applications in the sales world are endless.

GET THE ORDER RIGHT!

The critical issue here is that we take the appropriate steps in the appropriate order. When we give in to our discomfort, that order is as follows:

1. Discomfort

2. Decision

3. Action

I have made the case that when we reach a point of discomfort without having made a decision in advance, our first instinct is to run away. Being bold rearranges the order like this:

1. Decision

2. Discomfort

3. Action

If you are following CBT principles, you will choose the latter order, and it will make all the difference in the world. In fact, the remedies that follow will be based entirely on this approach. True, the execution is slightly more complex, but the structure and foundation are straightforward and simple to understand.

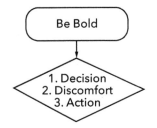

CBT EXAMPLE

Let's take a fictional sales professional—we'll call her Julie—and place her in an environment where she is selling cosmetics. Julie loves her products and appreciates it when her customers walk away feeling good about their experience with her. Cosmetics sales are emotionally driven. That is, people buy based on how the product makes them feel and, by extension, on how they feel about the product.

Julie loves the emotion-based sales and excels at talking to customers on emotional terms. What she does not enjoy is engaging with customers who are closed, distant, unemotional, curt, and sometimes even rude.

Because Julie sees a large number of customers in her department, it is inevitable that some of them will be less than responsive in their demeanor. In other words, Julie should be able to anticipate this attitude and plan for it in advance. The planning in this case will be to determine, *in advance of the discomfort*, how she will respond when she finds herself faced with the type of customer she doesn't enjoy.

Julie must make a decision (cognitive) as to how she will respond (behavioral), but she must do so *before* she is in her Moment of Discomfort.

WHY COGNITIVE BEHAVIORAL THERAPY WORKS

CBT is effective because it takes the emotion (or at least some of the emotion) out of the uncomfortable situation. Our primitive and instinctive reaction to discomfort is to run from it quickly and safely. We do this most naturally by running to our "comfortable place," but often that comfortable place is destructive, or at the very least self-limiting. We know this, of course, but we run there anyway.

Consider a different example, a salesperson (we'll call him Bill) who struggles with prospecting calls. As part of his company's directive, Bill has blocked out 90 minutes to call "warm leads." These leads are all from people who had previously provided contact information on the company's website, but who have not taken any further steps. Bill knows that there are good leads in the stack, gems waiting to be unearthed. He also knows that he hates making phone calls, preferring to deal face to face with new prospects who come into his showroom. He is intensely uncomfortable on the phone, and when those 90 minutes can no longer be avoided, his tendency is to retreat to his comfortable place: Facebook (or Jigidi, or Sudoku, or some other time-sucking activity). Or perhaps he justifies his non-calling session by focusing on something else on his to-do list. After all, there are other things that have to be done as well, right? Bill's natural desire to be comfortable wins out over what he knows to be true (he needs to make the calls) and best (doing so may well lead to more income for him). Our addiction to comfort, like all addictions, is not easily beaten ... even when we know better!

> *Destiny is not a matter of chance; it is a matter of choice. It is not a thing to be waited for; it is a thing to be achieved.*
> —William Jennings Bryan

Think about your New Year's resolution to work out and lose weight. You made the decision, and you had every intention of sticking with it, but you didn't factor in the discomfort in advance. You made the resolution without being honest about the fact that sacrifices would be required. So when it came time to work out and the discomfort roared, you cowered and retreated to your comfortable place: the sofa. ("I'd better start slowly, since I'm out of shape—maybe tomorrow.")

CBT has the power to take a complex situation and break it down into bite-sized pieces with small, easy-to-accomplish steps. When we break down a problem into small steps, it becomes simpler to understand. This also leads to a sense of mastery with regard to a specific point, providing a sense of control over something that before felt uncontrollable.

Back to Bill. The problem is that Bill sees his fears of telephone prospecting as a complex situation with a great deal of history and no easy solution, and he is correct. The objective, then, is not to avoid the problem at the time of the discomfort, but rather to plan for both the discomfort and the response *before it happens*. The discomfort will still be there, but a new response will have already been decided upon. Pain is inevitable; misery is a choice, correct?

Later in this chapter, we will break down the elements of this decision into some simple steps. Right now, we'll leave it at this: Bill must decide his response *in advance of the discomfort*. If Bill simply waits for the discomfort to arise, with no premeditated decision on his part, he will respond from the primitive, emotional side of his brain. And what will this part of his brain instruct him to do? *Run!* But if Bill chooses his response in advance of the discomfort, he will make the decision from his logical brain, a decision that will yield far better results.

Bill has two choices here:

Option 1: Wait for the moment and respond emotionally.

Option 2: Decide in advance that when it is time to make the calls, he will, in fact, *make the calls!*

Is it really that easy? Well, no. And . . . yes! There are steps that need to be taken, which we will address shortly. But you need to understand that this is a decision of the will, and the will can be persuaded. The boldest, most successful salespeople on the planet have the same choices to make as you and I do.

In thinking this through from his logical brain, Bill comes to a deeper question: what is the *right* thing to do? This changes everything. Suddenly there is a moral component to the decision. As Bill grapples with this question, several other considerations pop up:

- What is my company paying me to do?
- What is in the customer's best interests?
- How will I feel at the end of the day based on how I handle this situation?
- What implications does this decision have for my personal paradigm and my confidence?
- What kind of salesperson am I?

For those of you who at this point are thinking that I have radically over-simplified the scenario, I have two responses. The first is, no, I have not. The second is, we can control only things that are under our control. Bill cannot control how his prospects will respond to his calls, but he has 100 percent control over his own actions and efforts. All that is left now is for the situation to play itself out. The outcome has a much greater chance of success if Bill has decided on his response in advance.

Cognition is the decision; behavior is the action. In an interesting paradox, cognition affects behavior, which affects cognition. When Bill remains resolute in the face of potential discomfort, he proves to himself that he is capable of controlling his own emotions. This changes the way he thinks about future calling sessions. This will *always* be his choice, and as he chooses rightly, his confidence expands for the next similar occurrence.

> *I can decide in advance how I will feel*
> *about a given situation.*

Not only does cognition affect behavior (which affects cognition), but it also affects our feelings, *which, in turn, affect our cognition.* I can decide (a cognitive action) in advance how I will feel about a given situation. When I find myself adopting a positive attitude toward something to which I would normally respond negatively, I learn (cognition) that I have the power to similarly control my feelings in other uncomfortable situations. I am not Morpheus and you do not live in the Matrix, but there is definitely a blue-pill quality to CBT. If it helps you battle your addiction to comfort, go ahead and picture Laurence Fishburne in your head. As we have well established, there's a whole bunch of other freaky stuff going on in your brain, so why not add him as well?

A LIFE-OR-DEATH EXAMPLE

Several years ago, a friend of mine named Keith was on a church mission to the Philippines. It was a time of great civil unrest in Manila, and Keith found himself in the middle of a gun battle in the lobby of a hotel. Keith and his wife hunkered down while guns blazed and people were shot. He could hear the cries of the wounded and could sense that his life was in grave danger.

I asked Keith later about how he felt at that moment. "Keith, you could have died right then and there. Were you panicking?"

Keith's matter-of-fact response floored me. "Was I worried? Of course. Was I panicking? Not at all. I knew it was a dangerous place before I got on the plane. I figured that God had led me to the Philippines and, specifically, to this hotel lobby in Manila. If God guided me to this place, then it wouldn't say much for my faith if I second-guessed the move. And if I died, I would die in the exact place where I believe God had called me to be."

This is not a story about missionary work or about an individual person's faith. This is about a cognitive act to decide in advance how one might respond to his circumstances. Discomfort (yes, even massive discomfort) is inevitable. How we respond can always be our choice.

STEP BACK AND REFOCUS

I don't want to sell you on the idea that any of this is particularly easy; it is not. This is not a matter of just having a strong enough will. It's not about pumping up your energy and making an impulsive decision to fix everything that is wrong in your sales life. This is a long and slow growth process, a concept that is sometimes difficult to grasp in an instant gratification world, especially with the weight of sales performance expectations on your shoulders. But this movement toward sales boldness must be seen as a series of small successes over a long period of time. This is a journey more than it is a destination.

The good news (great news, actually) is that we can decide to accept relatively minor pain before it happens. It is helpful to understand that the pain we fear is rarely as strong as the pain we will eventually endure if we do not consciously choose change and growth.

In the next chapter, we will look at how to handle smaller everyday discomforts. Then we'll take a deeper dive into tackling the advanced forms of discomfort. And finally, we will look at getting our arms around the monster discomfort, that beast that mocks us from afar.

But let's walk before we run, shall we?

Questions to Ponder

- Consider a sales scenario in which your thoughts (cognition) determined your actions (behavior), even when you didn't "feel" like taking action. Why did you respond to your thoughts instead of responding to your instinctive feelings? What outcomes might you have experienced if you had listened to your feelings instead of taking action based on your thoughts? Would you have been proud to accept those outcomes?

- Go back to the concept of paradigm, purpose, and action discussed in Chapter 2. Do your thoughts primarily instruct your paradigm or your purpose? Or both? What does this tell you about the central importance and power of your own thoughts?

- What advantage do you gain by deciding in advance how to think, feel, and act in an uncomfortable selling moment? What small discomforts can you begin rethinking right now? What series of small successes can you create to dismantle that discomfort over time?

Now Try This . . .

It's time to revisit the three discomforts and decisions that you identified at the conclusion of Chapter 7. Write them down once again in the table on the next page. (Yes, the repetition is intentional.)

Next, take the time to reflect on two different experiences:

1. Think about the short-term pain you may experience as a result of your decision for boldness. Use descriptive language that expresses your feelings. It might also be helpful to contemplate how long you would experience this short-term pain.

2. Now consider the long-term pain you will experience if you take the easy way out and yield in your Moment of Decision. Again, express yourself in terms of feelings, emotions, and consequences. Finally, take time to note how long you will face the pain and consequences of the comfortable choice.

Discomfort	Decision	Short-Term Pain from the Bold Choice	Long-Term Pain from the Comfortable Choice

Expert Interview: Brian Tracy

In addition to the body of work he has created in the area of personal development, Brian Tracy is the reigning international expert on sales skill development, with millions of followers around the world. He has authored more than 50 (!) books and has spoken in more than 100 countries.

On a personal note, I would add that I have been a raving fan of Brian Tracy's work throughout my career, and I owe much of my own success to his influence.

How important is confidence as a sales attribute?

I think self-confidence is the single most important quality for success in any field, but this is especially true in a field where you risk rejection and failure every time you open your mouth. Salespeople should expect to be rejected nine times out of ten before they find an interested prospect.

When I was young, I was terrified of speaking to people, terrified of even going up to a door. In time, I learned that a no doesn't mean that the customer is rejecting you, and that fear is a normal, visceral reaction. That kind of snapped it in place for me. I realized that rejection wasn't personal, so I just smiled through it.

Is self-confidence something that's in one's DNA, or is it a skill that can be developed?

I have taught selling to two or three million people, and I've also taught public speaking around the world. They are very similar. Everybody starts out afraid. Everyone is nervous because of a variety of psychological factors. But, over and over, I've seen people overcome their fears. I believe that self-confidence is a learnable skill. You can learn to be bold and courageous by simply doing the things you would do and engaging in the behaviors you would use if you were already bold and courageous.

There is a law of reversibility in psychology that you don't hear much about. We all know that if you feel confident, you will act confidently. But the law of reversibility says that even if you don't feel confident, if you act confidently, that action itself has a reverse effect that will cause you to feel confident. It's an interesting paradox.

Is that partially because when you appear to be confident, you find that people around you respond positively, and that, in turn, gives you energy?

Absolutely. The hardest part is the first part—taking action. It's like picking up a telephone to make a call, knowing that the chances of negativity and rejection are extremely high. You look at the phone; you walk around; you look at the phone; you get a cup of coffee; you look at the phone; you review your notes; you look at the phone. . . . But as soon as you pick up the phone and make the call, your fears start to disappear. The hard part is the anticipation. That's why you need to take the Michael Jordan, Nike approach and "Just Do It."

Technique is important in sales, of course. But a big part of success is how we see ourselves, and whether we see ourselves as being worthy of bringing a high level of value to any sales scenario. How much of sales success is based on our self-perceptions?

I've taught this for years under the banner, "Mental Programming for Sales Success." In selling, it is critical that we really believe in our product and its goodness, that we really believe that it will improve the customer's life, and that we believe all of this at a fundamental level. This belief drives the sense of value that we bring to customers.

In a University of Chicago study, it was shown that a salesperson's conviction about the goodness of his or her product is the most powerful psychological factor in the sales process. Customers are affected at a subconscious level by a salesperson's own subconscious conviction. This all occurs on a deep, emotional, almost intuitive level.

I was sitting with a woman the other day, and she was explaining her product. She wasn't trying to sell it; she was explaining the goodness and the value and the benefit of it. By the time she had finished explaining—two or three minutes—I wanted to whip the product out of her hand, and so did the people around me. That response was based solely on her conviction.

Two other things with regard to self-programming. First, the person you see is the person you will be. If you see yourself as a top professional—calm, confident, relaxed, positive, optimistic, and cheerfully selling an incredibly valuable product—and you feed that picture into your mind, it will feed your subconscious so that you'll behave that way in sales situations. Second, the way you talk to yourself controls 95 percent of your emotions, positive or negative. And the most powerful words you can use are, "I can do it," over and over again. Prior to any call, with any prospect, using any closing technique, say, "I can do it."

These words are like an internal pile driver. Each time you say them—"I can do it. I can do it. I can do it!"—you drive this belief deeper into your subconscious. At a certain point, you hit bedrock, and it locks in place in your mind. All successful people are people who believe in themselves. Just keep saying to yourself, "I can do it. I can do it. I can do it." You can do anything you put your mind to. And the great part is that this repetition acts as a weighted scale: as your confidence goes up, your fears go down. Eventually, your self-confidence overwhelms and replaces your fears.

Big Problems in Little Packages
Handling Everyday Discomforts

The secret of living a life of excellence is merely a matter of thinking thoughts of excellence. Really, it's a matter of programming our minds with the kind of information that will set us free.

—CHARLES R. SWINDOLL

THE BIG IDEA
Short-term success and small victories add up to big wins over the long run.

A s you have journeyed along this path of discovery and introspection, you have probably identified sales discomforts of all shapes and sizes. Some are relatively modest, leaving you feeling somewhat embarrassed to even call them "issues." Others are monstrous, out-of-control ogres that hamper your productivity and prevent you (or so you suspect) from reaching the top of the sales charts. Let's start at the very beginning—a very good place to start, or so I'm told.

HOW THIS BOOK ALMOST NEVER GOT WRITTEN

In the summer of 2012, I attended the National Speakers Association annual convention in Indianapolis, Indiana. It's an incredibly uplifting convention, and the people I meet there are always helpful and kind. Most important, the content from both the keynote speakers and the breakout sessions is rock solid.

On Monday afternoon, I attended a session that focused on how to get a book published, led by prolific author and speaker Cyndi Maxey. Cyndi has had six different business books published; clearly, she is an expert on the topic. I had written three books up to that point and had self-published each of them. With total sales of around 15,000 copies, I was very satisfied with the results, but I still dreamed of getting a book published by a prestigious publishing house.

Cyndi was amazing. I was inspired by every word she spoke. It was one of those sessions where I was getting more than good content; I was getting a major dose of motivation to go with it. I found myself on the edge of my seat, captivated by the very possibility of success in this endeavor. It was the old adage come to life: "When the student is ready, the teacher will appear."

At 4:55 that afternoon, I was back in my hotel room, knowing that I would be leaving on a 6:00 a.m. flight the next day (working with a client in another midwestern state). I was replaying the breakout session in my mind, and my motivation had not died down in the least.

I was struck by this thought: "I need to call Cyndi Maxey."

I was immediately struck by another thought: "I'm uncomfortable about doing that."

So here I was in my very own Moment of Discomfort. You will recall that I have telephone hang-ups, and I don't like rejection any more than the next guy. And it's 5:00 p.m.—she probably has dinner plans. And why would Cyndi

Maxey want to talk to me, anyhow? She has no idea who I am. And she's probably exhausted after her presentation. And . . . and . . .

Are you hearing that progression in my mind? I've been talking about it
for the entirety of this book.

Moment of Discomfort—Moment of Decision—Chase Comfort—Rationalize

Do you see it? That is *exactly* what I was doing.

And then it hit me: the absolutely vibrant irony of the situation. I realized that I was standing in my hotel room, uncomfortable about calling Cyndi
Maxey to talk to her about my authoritative book on doing uncomfortable
things!

I had to chuckle at just how far I had yet to venture on this journey. But
I also realized something vitally important right in that moment: "If I do not
pick up the phone and call Cyndi right now, *I will be forever disqualified to
write the book!*" Seriously, I could not in good conscience write a book about
overcoming discomfort and simultaneously feed my own addiction to comfort.

I made a decision and used my own method (which follows later in this
chapter) on this one. I decided in advance how I would feel when I made the
call. I created a new story to combat my telephone fears. And I played out the
call in my mind a couple of times.

Then I dialed the phone. The result: voice mail.

Yes, voice mail! Now I could say, "I did my part," without having to
actually talk to her. How sweet is that? I was feeling satisfied by having done
the right thing, but deep down, I was worried that the window of opportunity
had closed.

Five minutes later, Cyndi called me back. I raved about her presentation
and shared my enthusiasm, and then I basically begged her for a few minutes of
her time. We met in the lobby of the JW Marriott 10 minutes later. I learned in
short order that Cyndi is just a giver; it is in her DNA to help others.

I admit to being extremely nervous when we first sat down. I mean, what
if she didn't like the concept? No one wants to be told that his baby isn't very
attractive. But I plowed on with an enthusiasm that was not fabricated in

any way. I boldly shared my passion for the subject of boldness . . . and Cyndi caught the vision.

We spoke for an hour, lining up some key concepts and strategies. Cyndi walked me through the path of what to expect and how to get around obstacles. We laid out specific actions, and I ended up with clear marching orders.

It was one of the best hours of my professional life, and I floated out of the room.

Over the weeks that followed, Cyndi helped me develop a proposal that landed me an agreement with a literary agent, and subsequently a publishing contract with none other than McGraw-Hill Professional, the premier publisher of sales-oriented books in the world.

I want to point out that this entire exchange hinged upon one single Moment of Discomfort: would I call Cyndi Maxey? And that, my friends, is how it works. These single moments can define our entire careers.

THE BIG PROBLEM WITH SMALL DISCOMFORTS

As I look back at that incident with Cyndi Maxey, I am struck by how seemingly small a moment it was. In fact, these moments are so common that we often are scarcely aware of their existence.

The biggest problem with small discomforts is that they are so common that they can seem inconsequential. Nothing could be further from the truth. It is in exactly such moments that we make (or destroy) our sales careers.

If we are going to do something about this problem, then we have to start by evaluating the way our brains address these discomforts. The fact is that our brains operate on autopilot much of the time, consciously handling only the toughest of the tasks that come our way. Everything else is dealt with automatically and systematically, according to our programming.

The problem is that those autoresponses are so, well, automatic that we don't even think about them. They just happen, seemingly on their own.

(For a thorough understanding of how the brain deals with discomfort, I strongly recommend Nobel Prize winner Daniel Kahneman's book *Thinking, Fast and Slow*. His explanation of how our brains work in "systems" [System 1 and System 2] is very insightful and exceedingly applicable to the sales professional.)

> *We must begin by identifying those small Moments of Discomfort and then working to reprogram the autoresponses.*

We must begin by identifying those small Moments of Discomfort and then working to reprogram the autoresponses. In attacking the small moments, we will take a two-pronged approach:

1. Use the principles of cognitive behavioral therapy (CBT) to attack in advance of the uncomfortable but predictable situations.

2. Train ourselves in new autoresponses to the Moments of Discomfort that jump up and surprise us—those that we have no way of knowing about in advance.

Both methods are effective, and, in fact, both are necessary. But both are also exceedingly beneficial in helping you grow your "boldness muscle." When you handle the small but important discomforts, you will find:

- Short-term success and small victories that add up to big wins over the long run

- Increased confidence in your ability to master your own discomforts

- Growth of the "boldness muscle" that allows you to lift "heavier weights"

- Uncomfortable things becoming comfortable to you, paving the way for attacking the next larger discomfort

Don't discount that last point. If you want permanent, lifetime growth, you must learn that the path is down the road of discomfort. When we are no longer uncomfortable, we are no longer growing!

THE STRATEGY

Some discomforts are relatively modest; others are monsters. I recommend that you start by tackling the simpler discomforts first. Remember, we are trying to build your boldness muscle, and you only do that a little at a time. Go back and review your list of discomforts from Chapter 3. Refreshing your memory will make the steps far more applicable.

I will offer three distinct approaches to overcoming your discomforts. The first will focus on how to handle the smaller things, the second centers on handling "surprise" discomforts that sneak up on us, and then we'll take on the monsters.

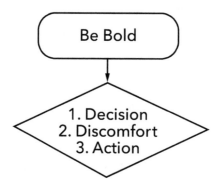

Let's start with a simple and direct path to dealing with predictable, everyday sales discomforts. Note that there is a huge difference between *simple* and *easy*. I would encourage you to look at this not as doing the *hard* thing, but as doing the *right* thing. Listen to your moral center. Heed the voice that instructs you to overcome your discomforts. You will know that voice if you listen carefully.

Just to refresh your mind, here are some categories of relatively minor discomforts:

- Introducing yourself
- Basic probing questions
- Price discussions (especially early on)
- Common objections
- Handling discount questions
- Awkward pauses in the conversation
- Staying positive when dealing with negative people
- Writing thank you notes
- Paperwork/administrative tasks
- Updating a CRM system

THE SIMPLE PATH

Here are the steps in the simple path.

1. Anticipate the minor discomfort in advance.
2. Decide in advance how you will respond.
3. Make up a new and positive story for the situation.
4. Play out the story in your mind over and over again.

I will elaborate on each of these, but it might be worth taking a few moments to focus on those steps and consider how you might apply them to your identified discomfort.

Step 1: Anticipate the Minor Discomfort in Advance

As I have already suggested, most discomforts are easily anticipated if you really stop to think about them. You *know* the moments that make you ill at ease, and you can be reasonably certain as to when these moments will occur.

However, when I say "anticipate," I am asking you to really place yourself in that moment. Feel it. Breathe it in. Don't evaluate the moment clinically, but rather step into it and experience what it is like to truly understand that discomfort.

Consider the discomfort in a price objection (if you find such situations uncomfortable). Put yourself in that moment when you think everything is going swimmingly, but suddenly your prospect claims that your product is dramatically overpriced. Think about your emotion. Are you feeling defensive? Are you concerned that the balance of power has just shifted dramatically? Are you squirming and uncomfortable?

Now consider the timing. When does that price objection come up? What happens in the typical sequence that would cause you to believe that such an objection could be on the way? How do you anticipate that before it happens?

I am asking you to take part in this mental exercise so that you can train yourself not to be taken by surprise. The surprise brings about an emotional reaction, and when we listen to our emotional voice, our "flee instinct" is activated. Being prepared for such moments allows us to call on our logical, rational brains.

It's OK if you're a little shaky at this point. That nervousness is a sign that exciting opportunities are ahead.

Step 2: Decide in Advance How You Will Respond

You may be noticing the common theme: "in advance." If you recall, the principles of cognitive behavioral therapy suggest that the decision (cognition) comes before the action (behavior).

When you think about it, your customers do this all the time. A couple pulls into a car dealership. Before they get out of the car, the husband leans over and says, "Honey, we're not buying a car today, no matter how slick this salesperson is and no matter what he throws at us. You got that?"

Can you imagine that happening? Of course you can; you might have done it yourself. Let's break it down. He made a decision (cognitive) in advance of the action (behavior). He might have sensed in his gut that buying a car is an emotional experience and that if he waited to make the decision until he was asked for it, he could make a mistake. The predecision is his way of controlling what he can control. And it is CBT in action.

- Anticipation of discomfort: being sold a car that he might not be ready to purchase.

- Decision for response in advance of the encounter: "We're not buying, no matter what happens."

- A predetermined action is in place *before* the emotional experience of falling in love with the car.

You can do the same thing, only make it a positive decision. Because the Moments of Discomfort are real and predictable, you can place yourself in that winning position in your mind. You can decide in advance how you will respond to those discomforts.

Let's go back to the grumpy prospect once again. You know that from time to time, you are going to get people who are less than kind. When it comes to big-ticket, emotion-based buying environments (purchases of homes, cars, boats, and the like), the prospect is scared to death, and the grumpiness is a manifestation of that fear.

The question is, what are you going to do about it? Are you going to allow the negative energy to deflate your own spirit a little, or are you going to stay strong and positive, no matter what negativity is thrown at you? You can make that choice, but you must make it before the moment arrives.

This is your decision. Eleanor Roosevelt once said, "No one can make you feel inferior without your consent." You can decide—*in advance*—how you will feel and, more important, how you will respond.

Step 3: Make Up a New and Positive Story for the Situation

> I skate to where the puck is going to be, not where it has been.
> —Wayne Gretzky

Your old comfort-chasing behavior comes with its own built-in story. Just as smaller discomforts are so routine that accepting them becomes normal for us, so too do the stories we tell ourselves become a normal and accepted part of our mental dialogue.

- "He wasn't going to buy anyway."
- "People don't like it when I ask too many questions."
- "I'll just tell him the bottom line; he's going to figure it out eventually."
- "No one even cares about thank you notes. They're just junk mail."

My friend, you need to rewrite the story, and you need to replace it with a new story *before* you get to the Moment of Discomfort.

Let's suppose that you are struggling with a common objection; call it a price objection. You might be able to negotiate a little bit on the price, but it will come out of your commission, and your company wants you to hold firm. Your inner voice tells you to hold your ground; your desire for comfort instructs you to give in and offer a discount.

You need a new story, something like this:

My product is worth every penny; it represents an outstanding value for our customers, and suggesting a discount will only cheapen the offering. I'm better than that.

Now, you're not just saying that, of course. You have to believe it. But you also have to reprogram your mind to believe it *fully*. This is why repetition is so important in the training process. You have been repeating negative thoughts for years, even decades. Those negative thoughts (stories) need to be trained out of your brain. The only way to do that is to force new and positive stories to take their place, and this can be done only by repetition.

SELF-TALK: VALID TACTIC OR HOCUS-POCUS?

I admit to having a cynical streak. While I live in the world of performance improvement, I tend to look skeptically at self-help techniques; thus, I have always struggled with the question of self-talk. Is it a valid technique, or is it just temporary, feel-good tripe? ("I'm good enough, I'm smart enough, and, doggone it, people like me!")

During his presentation, a speaker friend of mine suggested self-talk as a worthwhile pursuit. I challenged him after the speech, sharing my skepticism of the practice. He asked me an interesting question.

"Jeff, do you ever do anything stupid?"

"Of course," I responded.

"And do you ever find that you are mad at yourself when you do?"

"Sure, don't we all?"

"And Jeff, what do you say to yourself when you are not pleased with your own actions or behaviors?"

"It sounds something like, 'Oh, Jeff, you idiot. How could you be so dumb? What a moron.' That kind of thing."

"Okay, so you *do* believe in self-talk, just not positive self-talk."

Ouch. I was dead to rights and totally defenseless.

This lesson is important. In our society, *negative* self-talk is perfectly acceptable, but *positive* self-talk is labeled as silly, out of touch, and even dangerous.

The danger lies in the fact that we are what we continually think. Our self-paradigms are programmed over time, so that which we think about defines us.

Positive stories are a form of self-talk, and they must be repeated if they are to take hold. You must overcome your discomfort by telling yourself new and positive stories.

Step 4: Play Out the Story in Your Mind Over and Over Again

The mind is an amazing machine. It can take an incredibly complex instrument—your body—and direct it to perform spectacular feats. And the more focused the mind, the more incredible the end results.

Think back to when you were watching the Winter Olympics, specifically the downhill races or the luge competition. Before the race, the camera was often trained on one of the competitors who was locked in and focused on the race to come. What is an athlete doing at this point? She is racing down the course in her mind. Her eyes are closed, but her body is leaning into curves and quickly jerking back to the straightaway. She is mentally preparing for the race by visualizing her own success.

> *Golf is a game that is played on a 5-inch course . . .*
> *the distance between your ears.*
>
> —BOBBY JONES

Something incredible happens when we clearly picture the successful outcome of an action. The mind does not easily distinguish between natural reality and synthetic reality. This is the fundamental basis for virtually every idea. The newly formed idea exists in a future state based on a created story. The mind accepts the possibility of such a reality and runs with it.

This is not just a matter of repeating your story over and over again. It is about *feeling* the new moment in all of its pleasurable victory. It is the sensation of staring down your discomfort and capturing success.

And how great is that? You get the benefit of enjoying how you feel about conquering the discomfort even before you do so. Then you get that thrill *again* when you are successful in execution. Pretty cool, yes?

FOUR STEPS IN THE SIMPLE PATH TO OVERCOMING DISCOMFORT

Again, here are the four steps in the simple path.

1. Anticipate the minor discomfort in advance.

2. Decide in advance how you will respond.

3. Make up a new and positive story for the situation.

4. Play out the story in your mind over and over again.

May I encourage you to apply this progression *right now?* You will find the greatest benefit through immediate application. Pick a sales discomfort (or any other relatively minor discomfort, for that matter) and apply the principles immediately. Like now. As in . . . *do it*!

Questions to Ponder

- Consider the idea of "autoresponses" discussed in this chapter. Can you identify any autoresponses, either positive or negative, that are already programmed into your mind? Have you ever consciously (or even unconsciously) developed an autoresponse that was designed to help you deal with a difficult and recurring sales question? How can a conscious decision to design a positive autoresponse enable you to achieve small victories over your discomforts?

- When you think about anticipating a minor discomfort in advance, what are some ways in which you can mentally place yourself into the experience? What can you do to connect yourself with the emotions faced in that Moment of Discomfort? Take a moment to verbalize some expressive words that describe your experience when you are faced with one of your discomforts.

- What makes deciding on your response in advance such a powerful strategy? What are the benefits of this approach? Do you find it difficult to envision your decision in advance? Are you able to connect yourself with the positive emotions you will experience when you achieve a victory over this discomfort? Take a moment to verbalize some expressive words that you believe will describe your experience when you overcome one of your discomforts.

- Why is repetition such a key element of this simple path? How often do you think you will personally need to practice/repeat this simple path ahead of time in order to achieve victory in the Moment of Discomfort?

Now Try This . . .

Refer back to your list of three discomforts that you are dealing with right now. Choose the one discomfort that you see as the smallest of the three and write it in the following space.

_____

Next, take a few minutes to move through each of the four steps in the simple path. Use the space provided to write out your responses and plans for each step in the path.

1. *Anticipate the minor discomfort in advance.* When are you most likely to encounter this discomfort? What situations bring it about? How will you feel in that Moment of Discomfort? What thoughts will go through your mind?

_____

_____

_____

_____

_____

_____

2. *Decide in advance how you will respond.* Write out the most positive version of this experience that you can imagine. Include the decision that you will make and the action that you will take.

_____

_____

_____

_____

_____

_____

3. *Make up a new and positive story for the situation.* Why is this the right choice to make? What will be the outcome? How will you feel afterward?

_____

_____

_____

_____

_____

_____

4. *Play out the story in your mind over and over again.* How will you begin practicing, repeating, and replaying this decision path? Write down specific actions, times, and frequencies for mentally running through this path in the coming days.

_____

_____

_____

_____

_____

_____

Expert Interview: Khadeejah Johnson

Selling homes is tough work. I know; I did it for many years. It's even tougher when you are selling in a location that, shall we say, "has potential." But now add the fact that conventional financing is not available and the only available mortgage comes at a substantially higher interest rate. Did I mention that these are condominiums? In Harlem?

Enter Khadeejah Johnson, a 15-year home sales veteran who knows and loves a good challenge. Khadeejah's incredible sales success in Harlem real estate earned her the national honor of 2013 Salesperson of the Year by the National Association of Home Builders.

Tell me about the community you sold in New York.

It was a condominium community: 44 homes above the Aloft Hotel in Harlem. Harlem definitely carries a stigma, and that had to be addressed, but the area is in transition. It's a nice place to live.

What were the most difficult sales challenges you faced?

I really had two sales presentations. The first was in selling the home and the location. The second was in selling the financing. All we had available was an adjustable-rate loan that was higher than the prevailing fixed-rate loan. Customers really struggled with that idea. It took a lot of persuasion.

What is your secret for success?

I don't conform to the normal show-and-tell sales philosophy. I am very conversational. I want to have fun, and I want my customer to have fun right along with me.

Give me an example of what "fun" looks like in your sales presentation.

I was showing a home to a buyer who had a real estate broker with her. While we were on the tour, the broker was humming a song, so I joined in. Before you know it, we were both spontaneously singing full voice. The customer just sat there with her eyes big and a smile on her face. The broker had been working with her for two years and had shown her countless homes. Somehow I knew that I needed to take a chance and stand out.

How did you learn how to sell?

Mostly by trial and error, and eventually by trial and triumph. I started by leasing apartments when I was 19. My learning method was to throw it all against the wall and see what sticks. I tried as many approaches and techniques as possible.

In time, I learned that my greatest strength is my ability to be conversational. After a few minutes, customers don't know I'm a salesperson. I want to connect on a more personal level. I want to work as if I'm selling to my best friend.

How do you stand out?

For one thing, I am blessed with an exceptional memory. People really appreciate that. I ask about their family, and then I remember what they told me. I remember if they have dogs, cats, fish . . . whatever.

Second, I am well versed in a lot of things. I'm a curious person, so I can converse with people about a lot of different topics. I also know how to say "hello" and "goodbye" in a number of different languages. I have studied a variety of cultures, so I can speak to and from a wide range of perspectives.

When you first started in sales, what made you most uncomfortable?

It was always uncomfortable asking people to buy. Honestly, it still is from time to time. But now, my sense of obligation and commitment trumps my discomfort. I don't ask for the sale as something I'm doing for myself—I do it for them.

Repetition goes a long way toward reducing angst. I practice doing the same thing over and over again. I role-play a lot, and I try to pick the hard situations—really difficult people, for example—to play out in my mind. I've learned how to remain calm and trust the process. That way, when I meet a real prospect, I've already had the conversation with him or her that I want to have. It's stupid to try something for the very first time in real time with a real customer.

Do you find discomfort in role playing?

I do, but I also understand that it is an absolute necessity. I'm not nearly as uncomfortable as I used to be roleplaying, but that's because I do it a lot. I think it is the best possible way to improve my performance. And if I'm uncomfortable, that's a good thing. It means I have more work to do.

What makes you uncomfortable in sales today?

Cold calls. I hate them. That is a time when I get uncomfortable. I just don't think I can build rapport as well by phone as I can face to face. Even follow-up calls are uncomfortable if I suspect that the customer wasn't that interested. But I still do it. You miss 100 percent of the shots you don't take.

Handling the "Gotchas"
Developing Autoresponses for Surprise Discomforts

*The only thing that should surprise us
is that there are still some things that can surprise us.*
—FRANÇOIS DE LA ROCHEFOUCAULD

THE BIG IDEA
*You must do the uncomfortable thing as soon as you
sense the discomfort.*

The first and best approach should be to anticipate our discomforts and reprogram them with a positive response in advance, as described in the previous chapter. Alas, it's not always that easy. At times there are Moments of Discomfort that take us by surprise.

Recently, while I was presenting a half-day training workshop that addressed the topic of asking prospects deeper-level motivation questions without appearing to be nosy, it became clear to me that one particular sales professional simply did not want to be there. His body language was closed, and he shook his head from side to side throughout my presentation. He had no desire to even attempt to hide his distaste for the message. This doesn't happen often (at least, not to me), but this was a particularly difficult situation. Of course, we know that every Moment of Discomfort carries with it a simultaneous Moment of Decision. In this case, I had to decide whether to confront the salesperson during the break (uncomfortable) or just blow the situation off and keep going (still uncomfortable, but less so).

THE DANGER IN SURPRISE DISCOMFORTS

When we are thrown by an unexpected discomfort, we have a double concern to deal with:

1. The discomfort itself
2. The emotional trauma of being caught unprepared

It would be in our very best interests to have a method for dealing with unanticipated discomforts in mind, but I realize that it would be unrealistic to expect anyone to follow a "Four-Step Plan for Overcoming Unexpected Discomforts on the Fly." It might look good on paper, but it would never work in a real-life sales encounter.

> *The tactic must be simple, and it must be driven first by an attitude and then by a technique.*

The tactic must be simple, and it must be driven first by an attitude and then by a technique. If we can get the mindset correct, we will see our technique follow suit in the form of an autoresponse.

> Handling Surprise Discomforts:
> 1. Enjoy the surprise discomfort
> 2. Make up a new story

Step 1: Enjoy the Surprise Discomfort

This is going to sound like really strange advice, but I want to talk about how to make a seemingly ugly discomfort pretty.

Suppose you are mildly hungry and you head to the fridge. You find exactly one slice of three-day-old pizza. That slice of sausage, mushroom, and pineapple pizza was delicious when it hit the table, but today it is well past its prime. You make your decision: "That pizza looks nasty, and after all, I'm really not that hungry."

Now suppose you are on a hike and you get lost in the woods. You wander for three days before you stumble on a deserted cabin. By this point you are starving, and you go to the fridge and find . . . a slice of three-day-old pizza. Now what are you going to do? You scarf it down! And while you are inhaling that pizza, you notice something: it is the best-tasting pizza you've ever eaten!

The point is that the brain has the ability to define beauty on its own terms depending on the situation. You can choose to see discomfort as being ugly or beautiful, and that is 100 percent your call. Our primal reaction is to put discomfort into the "ugly" category. I suggest that it is time to rise above and rethink that.

Consider weight lifters. Those who are involved in serious resistance training will tell you that they anticipate "the burn," that moment when their muscles feel as if they were on fire. The burn is evidence that a workout is at its highest intensity. Muscle burn is welcome pain to a weight lifter, as it provides evidence of growth. In this case, pain (discomfort) is seen as a beautiful thing. No pain, no gain, right?

This is all a matter of perspective. How do you choose to see discomfort? How do you choose to deal with it as it comes upon you?

Notice the word: *choose*. You are not a helpless victim in the face of your own discomfort. You can—and you must—choose to respond in a more productive manner. The most productive manner of all is to choose to see discomfort as a beautiful thing.

I want to encourage you to find a way to make discomfort enjoyable. See it as a guiding friend rather than an adversarial foe. Accept and appreciate that the path to growth leads through your discomfort. As such, this should be exciting. Great things are right around the corner.

Look at it another way: if you have no discomfort, you are simply not trying very hard. Discomfort is the evidence of growth, or at least of the potential for growth. So when you feel the Moment of Discomfort, try this. Make a fist at shoulder level, then throw your elbow toward the ground and give yourself a fist pump and a mental "yes!" I know this sounds wacky, but think for a moment about the mental conversation: "Yes! I am uncomfortable, and that is the surest sign that there is a growth opportunity staring me in the face." I believe you would be willing to do this for someone else if it would help him or her to grow, so be willing to do it for yourself.

Step 2: Make Up a New Story

With your new attitude in place and your fist pump proudly performed, you must immediately tell yourself a new story: "I do the uncomfortable thing as soon as I sense the discomfort."

Make it a strong, positive statement. Breathe it in and believe it. That story will propel you to outstanding behavior and eliminate your negative voice.

Here are a few examples of positive stories. Pick the one that sounds the most like you:

- "When I sense discomfort, I smile. I understand that discomfort means opportunity."

- "Yes! I am uncomfortable. Where do I grow from here?"

- "Discomfort is my secret mental training weapon. It's time to get strong!"

Don't like any of those? Fine; write your own. The important thing is that you first deeply believe that discomfort is an indicator of a growth opportunity. There is simply no growth in the absence of discomfort. Once you have that belief solidly in place, you can proceed to write the story that works for you.

If storytelling sounds like a strange concept to you, it might help to learn that this method is a powerful component of cognitive behavioral therapy. Therapists work through cognitive distortions by replacing damaging mental language with powerful and positive countering stories. If you think about it, up to this point, you've probably been telling yourself and accepting negative stories; now it is time to exchange them for positive stories.

> *Repetition of the same thought or physical action develops into a habit which, repeated frequently enough, becomes an automatic reflex.*
>
> —NORMAN VINCENT PEALE

The story you create will need to be crafted into an autoresponse. If you have to think about it too much, you will probably allow enough time for a different story to seep in (and that story might say, "This is uncomfortable; run away!"). There is only one technique for developing an autoresponse: repetition. It would be wise for you to take the time to repeat your autoresponse *out loud* over and over again. (I know that sounds uncomfortable, but that's what this book is all about, right?) Write it down and post it in a prominent place. Keep it on your desk, or make it the wallpaper on your smartphone. Just understand that you have to revisit the message constantly in order to master its meaning. The destination called mastery is on the road called repetition.

This is all within your power, my friends. Embrace it. Feel it. Cherish it. You are not like the mediocre salesperson who shuns discomfort. You welcome discomfort as an opportunity to grow, and you greet it with a hearty fist pump, an enthusiastic "yes!," and a new and positive story.

I am fully aware that this might sound like hype and rah-rah; feel free to call it that if you are so inclined. Just understand that the alternative is to wallow in your safe little zone, victimized by your own limiting addiction to comfort. If you want to truly maximize your potential, that is not the path that will get you there. In fact, it is not a path at all . . . it is just a rut.

REVISITING THE SKEPTIC

Remember the salesperson who wanted no part of my presentation? I made a bold decision to confront him during a break. As it turned out, he was a fairly strong producer who had sat through one too many sales training sessions that had tried to get him to do things that were, in his opinion, manipulative and sleazy. He had made an unconscious decision to reject the message before the day had even started.

Interestingly, he was fairly pleasant to talk with one on one. I shared my concern that his visible rejection was having an effect on me and possibly on other attendees. He was taken aback. He really had no idea that his body language appeared that negative. He went on to say that he tended to process things through a negative skepticism, a sort of trial by fire of the material, but that he liked what I was saying. Hearing this confirmed my decision, uncomfortable as it was, to speak with him. Had I not been bold, I would have gone away from that presentation being "certain" of what this person had been thinking, and I would have been quite wrong.

THE BOLDNESS MUSCLE

It would be far too easy for you to simply nod your head and say, "Yes, Jeff, this all makes sense," but merely agreeing gets you nowhere closer to dealing with your discomfort. You know instinctively that you do not build muscle mass by thinking about exercise. In the same way, you do not build the boldness muscle by reading a book. You must take part in a workout routine.

Embrace surprise moments as opportunities. Give yourself the fist pump. Tell yourself a new story on the fly. Then tackle that bad boy head on!

Boldness is, in my opinion, the most underrated (and arguably most misunderstood) of all the sales attributes. Remember our definition as you continue to work on building this muscle. Boldness is not about being pushy or abrasive or manipulative. Boldness is doing the right thing regardless of your level of discomfort or fear.

Be bold, my friends. The world needs you.

Questions to Ponder

- Can you think of a time when you found yourself surprised by an *unexpected* Moment of Discomfort? How did it sneak up on you? What was your attitude? How did you respond?

- How can you train your brain to embrace, enjoy, and even celebrate a surprise Moment of Discomfort? What attitude will you adopt? What paradigm will you construct?

- Do you find yourself engaged in negative self-talk? How can you build a positive autoresponse for a surprise Moment of Discomfort? What aspirations will you chase? What affirmations will you give yourself?

Now Try This . . .

In the space given here, write down the positive autoresponse story you will tell yourself when you are surprised by an unexpected Moment of Discomfort:

_____

_____

_____

_____

_____

_____

The Advanced Course
Dealing with Big-Time Discomforts

Given the choice between the experience of pain and nothing, I would choose pain.

—WILLIAM FAULKNER

THE BIG IDEA
Overcoming your addiction to comfort requires immediate and automatic reactions. You master your automatic reactions through repetition.

The word *hero* is thrown around rather carelessly at times, but I think it appropriate to apply this moniker to one of the greatest salespeople of all time: Bill Porter. If you've never seen the movie *Door-to-Door: The Bill Porter Story*, I recommend that you rent it immediately. And if you can get through it without getting choked up, you can then explain what it's like not to have a soul.

Bill Porter was a door-to-door salesperson whose territory covered an incredibly hilly area of Portland, Oregon. It would be tough enough for a healthy individual to deal with the 10 miles of walking a day, carrying a large case of samples over seemingly never-ending hills. Imagine, then, what it would be like to do this if you suffered from cerebral palsy.

Bill Porter covered that route for the Watkins Company for more than 50 years. He was deemed unemployable, but he begged Watkins for a job and the company gave him its worst route. In 1989, Porter achieved Salesman of the Year honors at Watkins, and he was later recognized with an achievement award from the National Council on Communicative Disorders. He would have been out there for who knows how many more years, but in 1997, he was hit by a car while on his route and broke his back. No problem—he switched to telephone sales.

A *20/20* story on Bill Porter led to more than 2,000 calls and letters, the most for any story ever broadcast by that show. Clearly, the story hit a national nerve. Bill Porter himself is rather nonplussed by the attention given to his life. Asked in a 2002 *People* magazine article if he is ever surprised by what he has achieved, he responded, "It never entered my mind that I couldn't."

TAKING ON THE "BIG BOYS"

In the last two chapters, we looked at simple approaches to handling everyday sales discomforts, things like dealing with grumpy people, asking for contact information, or dealing with common objections. If only it were always that simple. In this chapter, we look at some of the more intimidating and challenging discomforts, those things for which there is no simple cure.

For example, when it comes to making prospecting calls, I could play the Nike card and say, "Just do it." But that approach won't work for a discomfort that you've been carrying around for your entire career. For the larger discomforts, there is reprogramming that must take place, a mental rearrangement of both paradigms and techniques.

> Nothing can stop the man with the right mental attitude from achieving his goal; nothing on earth can help the man with the wrong mental attitude.
>
> —ATTRIBUTED TO THOMAS JEFFERSON

It's time for you to take on your major discomforts. It is up to you both to decide and then to act upon your decision. This is the opportunity for life-changing actions on your part. May I challenge you to seriously consider the opportunity? Careers are transformed by such decisions.

I want to encourage you to read this chapter actively. As you learn the steps, I suggest that you apply what you can use as you go along. Take notes in a journal, and write out your strategy. The more engaged you are in the process, the more likely it is that you will take active steps when you face that significant discomfort.

You've probably guessed by now that this is not a book of fake cures and quick fixes. Overcoming our addiction to comfort is not easy. Hopefully, by this point, you have come to understand that developing a mindset that embraces discomfort is challenging, but in an exceedingly healthy way.

MY SALES DISCOMFORT JOURNEY

I confess to having a lifelong addiction to comfort that almost cost me my job early in my career. I joined the real estate sales industry at a time when the market was booming, and I would have told you at the time that I was the greatest sales professional ever to set foot on God's green earth. I was all that and the proverbial bag of chips.

Then the housing market fell apart and everything changed. Well, everything but me, that is. I continued with the same course of easygoing activities that I had pursued in a strong market, and that meant that I was waiting for the business to come to me. I called myself a fisherman, but I was just waiting for the fish to jump into the boat.

How bad did it get? It was the only time in my career when I got the dreaded 30-day talk: "Jeff, you have 30 days to figure this out, or you're going to have to find another place to work. And, by the way, no one is hiring."

That was the real start of my sales career. Up to that point, I had been masquerading as an effective sales professional, all the while knowing that I was following Daniel Kahneman's "law of least effort." I was doing the minimum necessary to get by, but not enough to be anywhere near great.

It was a turning point in my career. I was determined to go back to square one and learn the techniques that would launch me to success. More than 500 home sales later and after a successful stint in regional leadership, I found myself the national sales director for one of the largest home builders in the country, teaching others the very things I had learned in the trenches. And the most important lesson of all was, do the hard things that mediocre performers won't do. I systematically dismantled my desire for comfort and along the way launched a career that I have cherished for every moment since.

> *I made money in a time of prosperity. I learned how to sell in a time of adversity.*

I made money in a time of prosperity. I learned how to sell in a time of adversity. I could not have found success in any way other than embracing discomfort and radically reinventing my presentation.

DEALING WITH BIG DISCOMFORTS STEP BY STEP

As I walk you through this systematic approach to dealing with your tougher sales discomforts, I will use as an example one of the most universal of all discomforts: asking for the sale.

We all remember Alec Baldwin screaming his infamous "A.B.C." line: "A: Always; B: Be; C: Closing. Always . . . Be . . . Closing!" I don't know about you, but I personally found the scene to be more amusing than motivating. You can yell at me all you want, but it won't make me a more effective closer. Sorry. Old school is dead.

And yet in years past, closing theory has dripped with an ugliness that is stomach-churning. Closing has been taught as unapologetically manipulative by unscrupulous "trainers."

Asking for the sale is a topic that every sales professional on the planet has had to deal with at some point in his or her journey, and for many it represents a career-long battle with a personal desire for comfort. With this discomfort in closing come myriad examples of yielding moments and accompanying rationalizing stories.

I acknowledge that perhaps this might not be the most compelling example for you personally. Perhaps you feel zero discomfort in closing, and if that's the case, good for you. Feel free to pick another discomfort, but make sure you have something in mind before you proceed. This discussion will make a whole lot more sense if you are locked in on a specific area. And if you don't have any discomforts at all, well, I hate to break it to you, but you're not growing.

Let me lay out five steps to take in the face of serious discomfort.

Step 1: Make a Logical Decision About Handling Your Reaction to Discomfort

As I have repeatedly suggested, our greatest likelihood of success comes when we choose the response to our sales discomforts *in advance.* I would challenge you to think through your chosen discomfort and predict when you might face that discomfort next (and if that discomfort is asking for the sale, this should be easy).

Take some time to think this through on a purely logical basis. Reflect on past experiences and recreate the uncomfortable moment in your mind. Now ask yourself, what is the *realistic* worst-case scenario? It's time to ask for the sale, and what is the worst thing that can happen? The prospect might hit you in the face, or smear your heritage, or break down sobbing? Probably not. (And if something like that does happen, it probably had little to do with the actual question—something else went very, very wrong during the process.)

The key is to guard against what psychologists call "catastrophizing," the mental process of assuming the worst possible outcome of a situation. This is a type of thinking error, and it has no place in the mind of the bold sales professional. Assuming that you are a trustworthy individual and that you have built a respectable level of rapport, the *logical* worst-case scenario is that the customer will say no. That's it. Apply that premise to whatever your major discomfort happens to be.

Now come up with a rational response to the discomfort. Picture the likely scenario for how this will go down. Feel the no, and consider how you will respond to it. Feel the moment of rejection and contemplate how you might respond to the rejection and contemplate a healthy and positive reaction. Feel the honest reality of the situation.

I keep using this word *feel*. The more you prepare your mind with the pre-programmed emotional response, the more natural that response will become in the Moment of Discomfort. It is not enough to simply *think* about the moment; I want you to close your eyes and *feel* the moment.

> *We are battling the primitive "flee" instincts of your brain; we are overwriting the coding that works against you.*

Remember that we are battling the primitive "flee" instincts of your brain; we are overwriting the coding that works against you. This takes repetition, but it works.

Step 2: Rewrite Your Stories

Overcoming the addiction to comfort is about dealing with immediate and automatic reactions. Not only do we have a tendency to yield to our discomfort, but we have a tendency to yield *quickly*. The Moment of Discomfort and the supporting story all happen in a fraction of a second. Typically, there is simply no time to stop and shift from the avoidance of pain (emotion) to determining the right thing to do (ethics).

We learned in Chapter 4 that the stories we tell ourselves either are protective (if they are reactive in nature) or are groomed over the years (if they are recurring). The stories are as real as we want them to be. They are also as *false* as we see them to be.

The trick is to take control of our own automatic thoughts. To do that, we need to write new stories.

For example, one of my major discomfort categories is procrastination. That might not sound like it falls under the heading of "discomfort," but think about it a bit longer. Isn't procrastination simply avoiding the uncomfortable and putting it off for a while? Let me ask it this way: when it comes to a task or activity that you thoroughly enjoy, do you procrastinate? No, you don't.

My procrastination story typically sounded something like, "I'm busy now; I'll do it later." I got so good at that story that I didn't even have to think about it. The story was omnipresent.

My story has now been rewritten; the new story is: "I love the way I feel when I get things done right away." Bear in mind that this story is not just a load of self-help tripe. I really *do* love the way I feel when I get things done right away. Only now I visit that story in advance.

What is your discomfort story when it comes to asking for the sale? Here are some of the more common mental tales:

- "Customers will let me know when they want to buy."
- "I'm not pushy."
- "I don't want to ruin the relationship."
- "My product sells itself."
- "I like to let the sale flow more naturally."

It's time for a new story. Try this one: "I ask for the sale as a part of the service I provide."

The rationale for that new story is vitally important. If I do not ask for the sale, I am literally forcing the customer into the uncomfortable position of asking *me* for permission to purchase. I'm not talking about the stereotypical obnoxious closing line: "What's it gonna take to get you to buy my product today, little lady?" I'm talking about a comfortable, natural, and conversational invitation that makes it easy for a customer to buy my product: "I can see that you love this, and it looks as if it fits your needs perfectly. Would you like to make it yours?"

Automatic stories are learned by repetition. Don't think you can do this one time right here and then consider your addiction to comfort solved. These stories didn't appear overnight, and they won't go away quickly. You have to be diligent in your reprogramming.

Remember, the destination called mastery is located on a road called repetition.

> *As soon as we have the power to release our minds from the immediate here and now, in a sense we are free. We are free to revisit the past, free to reframe the present, and free to anticipate a whole range of possible futures. Imagination is the foundation of everything that is uniquely and distinctly human. It is the basis of language, the arts, the sciences, systems of philosophy, and all the vast intricacies of human cultures.*
>
> —Sir Ken Robinson, *The Element*

Step 3: Prepare for the Moment Just Before the Moment

To the extent that it is under your control, set up your success in advance. There are times when discomfort is thrust upon us, but more often than not, the discomforts that we face can be anticipated. Think back on recent discomforts that you have faced and ask yourself whether the moment could have been anticipated.

If you know it's coming, you can set up your success just *before* the Moment of Discomfort. Like an athlete who warms up and stretches just before an event, you can take a moment to affirm what you are about to do. This gives you a positive mental action while your resolve is strong. That last cognitive focus gets your fast-twitch mental muscle ready to fire.

In the sales process, you know the steps that lead to a closing question. Suppose you are selling automobiles, and you are on the test drive. You sense that this car meets both the needs and the budget of the customer. The customer is emotionally engaged in the experience. You *know* that a purchase decision is on the way while you are still on the test drive, and that it might occur the moment you step out of the car. In that scenario, you need to prepare for the closing question *before* you get out of the car. Make the decision as to how you will handle that moment up front. Play it out in your mind, and picture the warm, friendly, helpful, conversational discussion.

"Bob, Marianne—I always love it when I see someone fall in love with a car. This seems like everything you've been looking for. It would be my pleasure to help you with the purchase. Is that what you would like to do?"

Step 4: Isolate and Evaluate Each Moment of Discomfort

It takes time, energy, and perseverance to build a habit. But it also requires you to be a strategic student of your own presentation. The plan for boldness is not a one-and-done type of thing. We know that our discomforts will return over and over again. It seems prudent, then, to take a few moments after your sales encounter to reflect on how it went, but also to anticipate the next similar moment that lies ahead.

I am a lifelong San Francisco Giants fan, and the level of dedication that professional athletes display consistently inspires me. I am particularly drawn to the video review room, where professional baseball players will sit with the hitting coach and review their performance during their last at bat. They get feedback on their performance instantaneously, and they can apply what they learn in their very next attempt.

Each and every sales presentation is an educational opportunity. Specifically, we have a real-time occasion to evaluate our Moments of Discomfort and our subsequent responses. That sounds like simple advice, but it is not necessarily easy. Recall that our brains are wired to escape discomfort, so our natural desire will be to forget those moments quickly. That's a shame, because it is in these moments that our greatest learning awaits.

I want to encourage you to take some time and relive what transpired during a recent Moment of Discomfort. Consider the uneasiness and how you handled it, positively or negatively. Think about what you could have done differently. Right in that moment, commit to a better approach the next time around. Don't waste this glorious opportunity to coach yourself.

Beyond the evaluation, you must teach yourself that there is a training of the mind that takes place over time, and that this training is based on repetition. The good news is that each subsequent victory makes the mental muscle even stronger.

Again, use the weight-lifting analogy. When I start working out, I might be able to do eight curls at 15 pounds. As I get stronger, either I can increase the number of curls or I can increase the weight. At this point, if I go back and try to do eight curls at 15 pounds, representing the limits of my early discomfort, it will be downright easy for me.

But what if it's not a victory? What if, after evaluation and commitment to change, you feel that you have failed again in your attempt to ask for the sale (or whatever your major discomfort happens to be)?

When we focus on perfection, we will be forever frustrated. When we focus on progress, we feel invigorated.

That is all the more reason to evaluate what happened and to learn from it for your next encounter. Dan Sullivan, creator of The Strategic Coach® Program (a program that I am a very proud member of, by the way), likes to remind us all: "Focus on progress over perfection." When we focus on perfection, we will be forever frustrated. When we focus on progress, we feel invigorated.

The same is true as we train our brains to handle increasing levels of discomfort. The repetition makes us stronger, and eventually something that was quite difficult becomes relatively easy.

Step 5: Start a Victory Board

Enjoying the victory over discomfort is a choice that we can make every day as we systematically approach and embrace the moments we know we will face. I can and should be joyful about the fact that I am in control of my own response to my discomfort. I should celebrate the very idea that discomfort means conflict, and conflict means change, and change makes me a better salesperson. Above all, I can appreciate the fact that I am not a victim of my circumstances. It is my choice, and mine alone, to respond in a healthy manner.

Are you motivated to conquer your discomfort? Consider setting up a "victory board," a place where you can ceremoniously write down those specific moments when you embraced your discomfort and did the bold thing. It can be in the form of a journal, but I rather like the idea of being able to see those victories at all times. The constant reminder of my conquests builds my confidence and encourages me to continue in my pursuit. The victory board is an outstanding way to focus on progress rather than perfection.

So there you have it, five simple steps that you can apply today to any discomfort:

1. Make a *logical* decision about handling your reaction to discomfort.

2. Rewrite your stories.

3. Prepare for the moment just before the moment.

4. Isolate and evaluate each Moment of Discomfort.

5. Start a victory board.

FAILING SUCCESSFULLY, REVISITED

I want to revisit the idea of facing down our fear of failure. Fear of failure is just another category of discomfort, and, as with any other category, we have the capability to systematically dismantle this fear. If you are going to try anything at all, you risk failure—and that's a potentially beautiful thing. Failure means opportunity for growth and change.

Remember the premise: boldness is a skill set, and therefore it can be developed. But as when we are learning any skill—juggling, piano, carpentry, relationships, proactivity, *and sales*—this means that we are going to fail while we are in the process of learning. If that failure leads to our giving up, it is a disaster. But if it leads to our finding and fixing the problems, it is a wonderful victory.

Some discomforts are deeply rooted, and they will take time to overcome. Don't give up. Fail successfully—embrace the change and move forward. That is how you change the world.

> *Each problem has hidden in it an opportunity so powerful that it literally dwarfs the problem. The greatest success stories were created by people who recognized a problem and turned it into an opportunity.*
>
> —JOSEPH SUGARMAN

Questions to Ponder

- Why is it so important to make a logical decision about your response in advance of the discomfort? What happens if you wait until the Moment of Discomfort to determine your decision? Why is it also important that you feel the emotions associated with this decision?

- What is the relationship between your standards (what you are willing to accept) and your new stories? Similarly, how will your paradigm inform your new stories? Also consider the relationship between repetition and reprogramming; can you have one without the other?

- What steps can you take to prepare for "the moment just before the moment"? Are you connected deeply enough with your discomfort to plan for this properly? Similarly, what can you do to isolate the moment when it occurs? What level of awareness does this require of you, and how can you work to achieve it?

- Take a moment to think of three recent victories in your life. These can be sales-related or personal, and they can be big or small. Also keep in mind the idea of "progress over perfection." Now, why do you consider these things victories? What progress do they represent for you personally? How are you celebrating these victories day to day?

Now Try This . . .

Revisit the three discomforts you wrote down at the end of Chapter 7 and also the three decisions you wrote down at the end of Chapter 8. Decide which of these is your biggest and most challenging discomfort, and then write down that discomfort and the decision associated with it (again!) in the table below.

Next, write out your new story for that discomfort. Make sure your new story includes the following elements:

- Reflects the very best possible outcome imaginable.
- Defines a clear result or achievement.
- Aligns with your highest standards.

Discomfort	Decision	New Story

Now, in order to proactively prepare for this automatic response in advance, complete the two following statements using your own words:

I will prepare for the moment just before the moment by . . .

_____

_____

_____

_____

I will isolate and evaluate each Moment of Discomfort by . . .

_____

_____

_____

_____

Finally, chart your progress in "victory board" style in the coming days and weeks. Remember to focus on progress over perfection.

My Victories

Go!

*If you have three frogs sitting on a log and one
decides to jump off, you are left with three frogs.
Deciding does not get you off a log.
Jumping gets you off a log.*

THE BIG IDEA
Get uncomfortable if you want to get comfortable.

THE TRANSFORMATION

A few years back, I conducted a workshop in Bakersfield, California. It was a typical day for me, which means that I had expended a great deal of energy and was pretty much spent by the time I arrived at my hotel in the early evening. Speaking presentations that last for hours are tremendously draining events. By the time I got to the hotel, I just wanted to be horizontal as quickly as possible.

I checked in and walked over to the elevator for the ride to my third-floor room. A sign was taped to the elevator door: "Out of order. There is a second elevator on the far west side of the building, or you can feel free to take the stairs to your right." Moment of Discomfort—Moment of Decision.

I summoned my reserve of boldness for a quick pep talk. "Man up, Shore. It's two flights of stairs. How hard can it be?" I picked up my suitcase and computer bag and began the ascent.

By the time I got to my room, I was thoroughly gassed. Frankly, I could not believe how much that amount of exercise had worn me out. Fortunately, when I opened the door, I was greeted by a well-placed sofa. My bags hit the floor with a thud, and my body hit the sofa like a giant sack of laundry. Was I really in such bad shape?

Fortunately, the remote control for the television was within arm's reach, and I proceeded to do what guys do: channel surf. Someone once described the male television gene like this: "I don't care what's on; I care what else is on."

I was flipping through the channels when I landed on an infomercial and found that a man on the television was barking at me. At me!

"Are you fat? Are you out of shape? Are you tired by the simplest of exertions? Are you utterly exhausted when you've been speaking in Bakersfield and the elevator is broken and you have to climb two flights of stairs and collapse on the sofa in your hotel room?" (Eerie!)

The man on the television was Tony Horton, and the program was called P90X®. At one point in the commercial, Tony Horton looked at the camera and said, "Look at me—I'm 47 years old. If I can do it, you can do it."

That struck me because at the time, I too was 47 years old. Up to that point, I had kind of enjoyed being Jeff Shore, but at that moment, I wanted to be Tony Horton. And I could be—for only three easy payments of $39.95. That's nothing!

By the time I got back home several days later, I was fired up and ready to go. The DVDs were waiting for me, and I attacked them with vigor. Day one was chest and shoulders, and I gave it all I had. I found I needed to modify a few things, but I pushed hard.

By the morning of day two, I was sore in muscles I didn't know I had. The second day was all about plyometrics: jump training. After 10 minutes, I was gasping for breath. I just couldn't keep up.

On day three, we tackled legs and back. The pain in my quadriceps was like standing in flames. I began to hate Tony Horton and rue the waste of time and money.

By day four, I could barely get out of bed. Frankly, I was ready to quit, and I had plenty of stories to rationalize why I would do so. Still, I plowed ahead. I pulled out the DVDs to see what was on the agenda. I really needed a break, and I was pleased to see . . . yoga. I had never done yoga before, but really—how hard could it be to stand around like a tree for an hour? I learned very quickly how dead wrong I was.

I came very close to quitting the program that day, but I decided instead to skip ahead several weeks and watch the DVDs to see what was coming down the line. That is when I saw Tony Horton do something utterly amazing: a plyometric push-up. You know what a push-up is, of course. You've probably seen a clap push-up, where one pushes with enough force to clap one's hands before coming back down. A plyometric push-up requires enough force to get both hands *and both feet* into the air, clap, and come back down. That's right; Tony Horton was completely airborne.

This could have gone either way for me. I could have quit right there, knowing that I did not have it in me. Instead, I chose to embrace the discomfort in favor of the ultimate goal: my own plyo push-up.

It took me almost three months, but I pulled it off. It is a moment I will never forget. I had come so far and worked so hard for this one goal, but it was worth every drop of sweat from every workout.

Successes are like that. We remember most the things that we worked the hardest for. I poured a lot of effort, discomfort, and pain into that feat, so I will appreciate it for a long time to come. As I write this, several years later and in my fifties, I can still drop and give you 10 to 20 plyos on the spot, even in street clothes. Am I bragging? Yep! Why? Because I can.

YOUR OWN PLYO PUSH-UP

Tackling P90X is a story about dealing with discomfort. But it is also a story about how good I felt after I had done so. It is about the psychological victory and the rush of accomplishment. I was on a path to being out of shape for the rest of my life, but I made a conscious decision to overcome my desire for all things comfortable.

Do I still struggle with the motivation to exercise? Yep. Do I still want to tell stories to rationalize why I should stay on the sofa? Uh-huh. But I focus on progress, not on perfection. I count each battle as another opportunity for victory, and I remain in excellent physical shape today.

In the process of facing the discomfort of exercise, I developed a new realization: the benefits of dealing with the discomfort ran far deeper than I had originally thought. There is a far more significant reward at stake. And this is where it gets really exciting!

What is *your* plyo push-up? What challenge is out there, waiting to be conquered? What accomplishment would make you feel absolutely incredible? Do the hard thing. Embrace the discomfort. Work and push and sweat and even bleed a little bit if you have to; just do something incredible. What will that be? And why not today?!

BENEFITS OF BOLDNESS

Let's brainstorm about what is in store for you as you systematically and deliberately conquer your discomforts. What are the benefits? See the figure below.

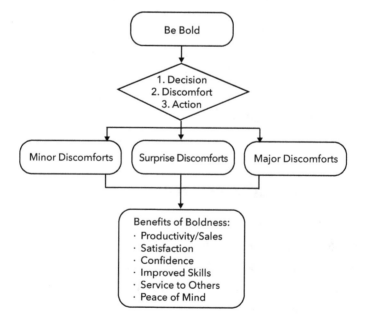

- **Greater productivity.** You get more sales. Surely you can see by now that the path to increased performance relies on your ability to leverage your discomfort and embrace the opportunities that lie within.

- **Satisfaction.** You feel better about your efforts, your performance, your results, and your life. You sleep better at night when you have taken each sales discussion as far as it could go.

- **Confidence.** Every discomfort conquered adds strength to the "boldness muscle." You can lift increasingly heavy weights.

- **Improved skills.** As you embrace discomfort and take significant action steps, you literally train yourself to higher levels of performance.

- **Service to others.** You are not the only one who is affected by your avoiding discomfort. You make the world a better place when you exercise boldness.

- **Peace of mind.** There is an indescribable contentment that comes along with putting forth your very best effort. You are a holistic creature, and a victory in one area of your life rolls into all other areas.

Look again. That's quite a list! But there is one more benefit that surpasses all of these; when I realized this, it was a game changer for me.

THE BOLDNESS/COMFORT PARADOX

You see, when I give in to my discomfort and take the easy path, there is a price that has to be paid. The guilt, the unrest, the knowledge in my gut that I copped out—all of these are crippling to me. I might gain a cheap, temporary, and unsatisfying level of comfort, but I know in my gut that I have not done the best thing.

But when I stare down the discomfort, leverage it, and make the bold move; when I look that moment in the eye and say, "Bring it!"; when I do what I know must be done, my single greatest reward is . . . *comfort!* Not the cheap kind of comfort that comes from giving in and taking the easy path, but *real* comfort. *Earned* comfort. *Lasting* comfort. It is the kind of comfort that causes me to hit the pillow with a smile on my face, and to wake up reinvigorated for the day to come.

> *If you look for truth, you may find comfort in the end: if you look for comfort you will not get either comfort or truth—only soft soap and wishful thinking to begin with and, in the end, despair.*
>
> —C. S. Lewis

It is an amazing paradox. Chasing comfort ultimately brings a false sense of comfort. Embracing discomfort and exercising boldness ultimately brings true comfort.

What are you doing to develop that kind of comfort? I encourage you to take action . . . *right now*. The journey is not easy, but it is incredibly rewarding. And it begins with a single step, a single commitment.

The ultimate benefit: you can change the world.

Questions to Ponder

- Have you ever had your own "plyo push-up" moment: choosing to tackle something big and then thinking about quitting? What path did you choose in that moment? How did you feel about your choice afterwards?

- How would you further define the "cheap comfort" that comes from yielding in the Moment of Discomfort? What damage does this cheap comfort create in your life?

- How would you further define the "real comfort" that ultimately comes from choosing boldness? What benefits does this real and lasting comfort provide in your life?

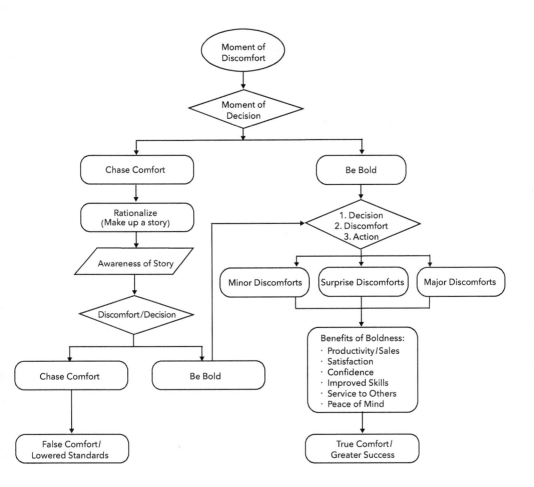

Now Try This . . .

First, review the "benefits of boldness" discussed in this chapter and shown in the following table. Take a few minutes to visualize and conceptualize what each of these benefits looks like in your life, both right now and in the future. For example, what would it mean for you personally to enjoy greater productivity? Think big, create from your imagination, and be specific.

Next, take time to summarize your conclusions in the column titled "What This Looks Like in My Life."

Consider copying or printing this table and displaying it somewhere that is highly visible as a future-focused touchstone that reinforces your daily decisions for boldness.

Benefits of Boldness	What This Looks Like in My Life
Greater productivity	
Satisfaction	
Confidence	
Improved skills	
Service to others	
Peace of mind	

PART III

PUTTING IT ALL TO WORK

THE CUSTOMER'S DISCOMFORT

Up to this point, I have laid out the discomfort–boldness progression from the perspective of the sales professional. Of course, there is a parallel level of discomfort at work here: the customer's discomfort in making a purchase decision and all that is associated with that process. It would be in our best interest to consider that path concurrently with our own. If we are to master the way we sell boldly, we must start by considering the way people buy. Make sense?

There is a fundamental flaw in far too many sales approaches. Many "critical path" sales models follow the selling path, but don't necessarily look at the *buying* path. Too often, there is a very specific script that both the salesperson and the buyer are expected to follow. Surely you have been in a training presentation where the message given was, "Now, when you say this, the customer will say that." There is only one problem: the customer has never been to the training.

Overly scripted presentations too often call for an "open wide; here it comes" approach. The sales performance is all about how wonderful the product is and how it will change your life. But this presumes that the sales decision is all about the solution. I would contend that the sales discussion first has to be about understanding the problem.

Let me make a bold promise: if you understand the customer well enough, the sales path will roll out right in front of you. The customer will literally show you how to sell him or her your product. This does not mean that you do not need to follow a sales structure, but rather that your structure must be designed in accordance with the buying pattern, not the selling pattern.

THE PROBLEM WITH THE "PITCH"

Consider what most people think of when you say the word *salesman*. They imagine a pitchman enthusiastically hyping a product for five minutes, seemingly in one breath. The visual that comes to mind is something like a Jack Russell terrier on Red Bull:

> Look at this product. It does everything you want it to do! It slices, it dices, it even makes julienne fries. And when you're away from home, it will scrub your toilets! One lady in Ohio swears it cured her gout. How much would you pay for just one of these devices? Don't answer, because if you order right now we'll give you *ten* for the price of one. No, you're not going deaf. It's 10-for-1. Why? Because we're crazy!

A bit over the top? Perhaps, but often it is only a matter of degree. Too many sales presentations follow a similar pattern of feature dumping, just in a toned-down version. That approach might have worked in the days when the salesperson was the only one who had access to all the critical information, but that was a different era.

In his book *To Sell Is Human*, Daniel Pink encourages a movement away from an attitude of "caveat emptor" (let the buyer beware) to one of "caveat venditor" (let the seller beware). Buyers' access to extensive online information has leveled the playing field and changed the very purpose of a sales professional. Says Pink, "Whether you're in traditional sales or non-sales selling, the low road is now harder to pass and the high road—honesty, directness, and transparency—has become the better, more pragmatic, long-term route."

"I HATE SELLING!"

A few years ago, I sat down to lunch with one of the most fascinating people I have ever met. Jim Adams is the founder and owner of NewHomesDirectory .com, and he bleeds boldness in just about every way possible. When Jim gets an idea in his head, he is as determined as anyone I've ever seen in pursing that dream. The success of his company is evidence of this fact.

At our initial lunch, Jim said something that intrigued me to no end.

"Jeff," he said, "I love everything about my job and my company except for one thing: sales. I hate the sales process."

Now, if you know me at all, you'll know that them's fightin' words. That statement had to be challenged. I asked Jim what was so disturbing about the sales process.

He replied, "Here's the problem. I get an appointment with a company, and I'll sit with them for 30 minutes. I'll tell them about the product, about its track record, and about why this makes so much sense. I'm as excited as I know how to be. At the end of the presentation, they say something like, 'We'll get back to you,' and that's it. Often I never hear from them again. I just hate being out of control."

I could spot the flaw immediately, and it had nothing to do with control. I offered Jim this advice: "Jim, the next time you have an appointment with a company, I want you to lead with this question: 'Why am I here?'"

Jim looked at me as if I had a hole in my head. I continued:

Jim, they're going to look at you like you're crazy. Just explain your question this way: "Look, you're busy people, and a lot of would-be service providers are asking for your time. You would not have agreed to meet with me unless something was wrong with your situation as it is. Let's talk about that. If I have a solution, I'll show you. If I don't, I can save you some valuable time."

Jim trusted me on this and took that exact approach with the next sales presentation he went on. The results were night-and-day different. Jim called me the next day, as excited as I have ever heard him.

"It was incredible! The 30-minute meeting went for 90 minutes. We spent the first hour just diagnosing what was wrong. At that point, the solution rolled out right in front of us. We signed them up on the spot!"

His sales presentation has never been the same, and now he loves the process.

Let me make a bold promise: if you understand the customer well enough, the sales path will roll out right in front of you. The customer will literally show you how to sell her your product.

Did you get that? If you understand the customer well enough, the sales path will roll out right in front of you. The sales path should be designed according to the buyer's needs. This is about discovery.

A "TOO-CLOSE-TO-HOME" EXAMPLE

A few years back, my daughter was coming home from college for Mother's Day weekend. She would make the seven-hour drive from Southern to Northern California in my pickup, an older truck that I had loaned to her while she was in college.

She arrived in Auburn, California, on Thursday evening while I was on a consulting trip in Virginia. I knew something was wrong when my phone rang in my hotel room at 9 p.m. California time, midnight on the East Coast. I knew it was even "wronger" when I noted that wherever she was standing, it was extremely loud.

"Katie, where are you?"

"I'm standing on Interstate 80."

"What?! What is going on?!"

"The truck died. I got to the side of the road, but I don't know what to do."

"Are you safe?" I asked.

"I'm fine. I just need to know what to do next."

Let me tell you as a father, this is not the call you want to receive from your daughter, and certainly not when it is your truck that she is driving. I confess that I was rattled by the experience.

We had the truck towed to our mechanic for evaluation. He called the next day with the bad news.

"Blown head gasket. Tore apart the radiator and a bunch of other stuff. It's over."

"Over?" I asked.

"Ain't worth fixing. The truck's not worth it. It's over."

I got back home late on Friday night. On Sunday, after church and lunch, Katie would be headed back to Southern California. Guess what we were doing on Saturday?

If you said, "Car shopping," you would be wrong. We were not car shopping on Saturday—we were car *buying* on Saturday. We left the house with the checkbook in our hand, and we knew that we could not return without a new car for my daughter.

Here is the million-dollar question: how important would it be for the salesperson to know my story?

We went to three different dealerships that day. Not one of them—not even one—bothered to discover why we there in the first place. No one took an interest in our situation. No one seemed to care that our situation was desperate. What did they want to talk about? Financing specials, limited time offers, and a whole lot of feature dumping.

I wish this were an isolated incident, but I think you and I both know that this is commonplace in the sales world. Salespeople everywhere are consumed with the solution . . . without really knowing the problem.

Look back a couple of paragraphs to where I asked a "million-dollar question." That is not hyperbole. Salespeople who do not understand the customer's story can literally leave a million dollars on the table over the course of a career.

I repeat: get to know your customers well enough and they will show you how to sell them your product.

THE CUSTOMER'S MISSION

I want to start with a very important premise. Every customer is on a mission, and we need to determine what that means.

Why does anyone want your product? Why would a prospect want to buy a recreational vehicle? Why would a client want to upgrade his life insurance? Why would a customer want a new sofa?

We need an answer that satisfies all those questions, so let's broaden the question: Why does anyone do anything? Why do we eat when we're hungry? Why do we date when we're lonely?

Every customer is on a mission—a mission to improve his or her life.

We are all motivated to improve our lives, and this defines our mission. Customers will buy your product when, and only when, they believe it will improve their lives. This implies that at some level, there is a certain discomfort that every prospect experiences, a discomfort of "incompleteness." That very discomfort nags them in the direction of a shopping experience.

Here is a simple example: consider the guy selling mops at the county fair. He shows you how incredibly simple his mop is to use. He rails about the insufficiency of your current mop. He paints a picture of how great your life will be as soon as you break out this new mop for the first time. In a simple way, this represents life improvement, and an alleviating of the customer's discomfort.

Every customer is on a life-improvement mission. Let me put that another way: if I don't believe that your product will improve my life, I'm going to pass on it. Why should I even consider a purchase if it will leave me no better off than I was before?

Your natural instinct at this point might be to say, "Well, gee, I'd better really spiff up my presentation so that customers can see how life-improving my product is." Hold that thought, if you would. Go there first, and you will miss a very important step.

DISCOMFORT FACTORS

There are four significant factors that direct a customer's mission, two motivators and two inhibitors. I will address these factors in the chapters that follow. For now, just understand that in the absence of life improvement, there is no sale. The customer has a potentially lengthy list of discomforts: discomfort with the need, discomfort with the choice, discomfort with the fear of the salesperson, discomfort with the cost, and so much more.

Our task is to understand these discomforts in order to prevent the customers from following the easy path and not buying our product. We need to make the discomfort of staying put more distasteful than the discomfort of moving forward.

There is a great deal at stake in this discussion. We have already looked at the perils facing sales professionals who suffer from an addiction to comfort. But what happens when a comfort-addicted salesperson meets a comfort-addicted buyer? The answer: *nothing*!

It is the job of the sales professional to help increase the customer's sense of current discomfort in order to present a better, life-improving future.

As we break this down into its component steps, I will ask you to keep your current customer base in mind. Let's see if we can't unlock the mystery as to why people are stuck on the fence.

The Customer's Mission
Current Dissatisfaction

*Too often we enjoy the comfort of opinion without
the discomfort of thought.*

—John F. Kennedy

THE BIG IDEA
The single greatest predictor of urgency is dissatisfaction.

THE IMPLICATION OF LIFE IMPROVEMENT

I have seven black dress belts. Seven. Who in the world has seven black dress belts? Well, I do. And it's not because I'm some sort of fashion connoisseur who collects belts the way Imelda Marcos collected shoes.

So why do I own seven black dress belts? Here's a hint: I bought six of them in hotel gift shops. Of course it makes sense now, right? The finest-quality dress belts are to be found only in hotel gift shops, correct? Or maybe it's because the prices are so incredibly reasonable that there is no way I can pass up such a great deal. No?

It's a mental block that I cannot explain, and I'm vulnerable every time I pack for a business trip. If I'm going to forget something, it will be a black dress belt. I'm stunned at my proclivity in this area.

I have stated that customers are on a mission, a mission to improve their lives. In the absence of a need for improvement, the customer buys nothing. Keep this concept at the forefront of your mind; it is critical.

Now ask yourself, "If people buy because of a desire to improve their lives, what does that imply?" It means that something is not right—that something needs to be improved. Or, if you will, that I am desperately in need of a black dress belt.

I define it this way: for every prospect you meet, there is a Current Dissatisfaction. Get used to that term; I'll use it a lot. The Current Dissatisfaction is the compelling motivator for action, as you will see.

> *In the absence of a current dissatisfaction, there is no need to buy anything . . . ever!*

All customers have a Current Dissatisfaction (I'll shorten that to CD going forward). If they didn't, they wouldn't be in your showroom. Why should they be? In the absence of a CD, there is no need to buy anything . . . ever!

On a recent business trip, I bought some very expensive shoes. Why? Because they were on sale? No. In fact, they were the most expensive shoes I've ever purchased. Because I loved the shoes? No. I loved them, but that wasn't my primary motivation. Why did I buy this pair of extremely expensive shoes? Because it was raining outside and I noticed that my socks were getting wet!

THE DISSATISFACTION SCALE

Dissatisfaction is prevalent in virtually every purchase decision. This is true because there is really no such thing as a perfect product. As consumers, we are always shopping for the best product in our price range. Or did you really think that every single person who is driving a Kia is behind the wheel of his or her absolute dream car? I've got nothing against Kias; I'm just pointing out that we drive the best car we can afford, not necessarily the perfect car. You were at least modestly dissatisfied with your old car when you started your last car search.

In fact, you can place your own dissatisfaction on a scale right now. Think about the car you are driving today (and if you don't have an automobile at present, just use your imagination). There is something wrong with your car. It might be a petty annoyance—a rattle or a dent. Maybe it's the cost—the payments are killing you. Perhaps the car has mechanical problems and you suspect that it could go at any minute. Or maybe it's just that unidentifiable odor.

Whatever the case, the issue leads to a scalable dissatisfaction, as shown in the figure below. In this case, a 1 means that you are actually very happy with your car, and a 10 means that you are standing in a dealership as you read this. So a 1 means that you are quite satisfied, and a 10 means that you need a new car and you need it right now. If you do not currently own a car, rate the dissatisfaction of the situation; 1 means that it's no big deal, and 10 means that it's a major life inconvenience.

The Scale of Dissatisfaction

Low	Moderate	High	Raging

1   2   3 | 4   5 | 6   7 | 8   9   10

This scale is a very important indicator of your buying pattern. The higher the dissatisfaction, the greater the need, and thus the greater the level of urgency.

DISSATISFACTION = URGENCY

Make no mistake about it: the single greatest predictor of urgency is dissatisfaction. It's not your awesome product or your incredible deal or your superior financing. It's not even your silky smooth sales presentation. The single greatest predictor of urgency is dissatisfaction.

Think about that for a moment. Have you ever been so hungry that you surprised yourself with what you were willing to eat? You go to the refrigerator and open it up to see what you can find. Nothing. So you close the door, wait two minutes, lower your standards, and open the door again. Finally you settle for the pickle in the jar that hasn't been opened since the Reagan administration.

Suppose you read a story about the latest technological advances in television sets. You are impressed with all the bells and whistles, the high definition, the integrated high-end speakers, and the Internet compatibility. But what if you were perfectly happy with your existing set—would you be in the market? You would not.

Every single potential customer carries with him or her a degree of dissatisfaction—every single one. That CD can be placed on a scale. A 1 means that the customer is actually quite happy with what he has; a 5 means that she is moderately dissatisfied but not entirely unhappy; a 10 means that things are seriously lacking and the customer has no choice but to purchase.

So if you are very happy with your car and have no desire to upgrade it, you might be in the 1 to 3 range. If the car is starting to get old and doesn't have the bells and whistles of the new models, you might be 4 to 6. And if your car is just downright distasteful to you—if you've completely fallen out of love with it—you might be in the 7 to 9 range. But if you parked your car in the wrong place yesterday and a crane fell on it and totaled it, your CD is at a 10!

In other words, a Level 10 CD means that you have no choice; you have to move forward. You will recall my daughter and my car buying during her short trip home, the day before Mother's Day.

CURRENT DISSATISFACTION = DISCOMFORT

Up to this point in the book, we have examined discomfort from the perspective of the salesperson. But we need to consider that there is a corollary discomfort on behalf of the customer.

Remember that the mission to improve one's life is initially based on a CD. Dissatisfaction is itself uncomfortable, so the customer is in something of a dilemma right out of the gate. Does he stay where he is, or does he move forward with a new purchase? His current situation is *comfortable* to him because of its familiarity, but it's *uncomfortable* because of his dissatisfaction with it. As sales professionals, we have the task of helping our customers develop the boldness they need to move forward with a purchase decision.

Don't lose sight of the fact that comfort is a compelling factor. "Doing nothing" is always an attractive option for almost every customer. When you hear prospects say, "We want to think about it," you are in a dangerous position. The battle you might be facing is whether they will maintain the status quo and stay with what they have. Your greatest competitor is not another supplier—it's what the customer has now. Here's why.

How Stress Affects Decision Making

In my research for this book, I asked a psychologist about the effects of stress on the decision-making process. For a customer, there is always a certain amount of stress associated with a purchase decision, especially for a big-ticket purchase. I wanted to understand how the presence of stress affects the buying process.

My question was straightforward: "How does stress affect decision making?"

The psychologist answered succinctly and surprisingly with these three words: "Stress constricts creativity." He expanded upon that concept with a layman's clarification: stress makes us dumber. It seems that stress has a tendency to cloud a portion of our brain, the part of the brain where creative thinking takes place.

Here is a very simple example. Suppose you are at a wedding reception, a cocktail party, or some other social event. You see someone walking toward you from across the room. You know the person, but you cannot remember her name. Your mental dialogue goes something like this:

"Oh, here comes . . . here comes . . . oh, come on. That's, um, . . . she's the one who knows that other guy . . . we met at the thing . . . she's getting closer. C'mon, think! What is her name?"

Good luck. Stress makes clarification harder to come by. You won't remember her name until your stress level decreases, which of course will coincide with the moment when she has left the building. ("Frances! Of course!")

A prospect's discomfort causes him or her stress, and that stress will constrict the prospect's creativity.

A prospect's discomfort causes him or her stress, and that stress will constrict the prospect's creativity. When creativity is constricted, we revert to decision making from a lower center of our brain. In times of stress, we crave simplicity, comfort, and familiarity. This is why people smoke or drink when they are stressed; they know it is not healthy to do so, but they are driven by their desire to relieve the discomfort of stress. Not only is an alcohol- or nicotine-induced soothing comfortable, but to the abuser, it is also predictably familiar.

When we are stressed, we go to the most comfortable internal place we know. That place is usually staying with whatever we have right now. Can you see how no action might be your single biggest competitor? On the one hand, if customers are dissatisfied with what they have, that makes them uncomfortable. On the other hand, the idea of change itself is problematic for many people, so moving forward with a purchase decision is also uncomfortable. At the end of the day, unless there is compelling evidence that moving forward will be less painful than staying put, the prospect will chase comfort and not make a purchase decision at all.

That's the bad news. Here's the good news: if their dissatisfaction is high enough, the customers simply cannot stay where they are. They have to move forward (and buy something). That is what this chapter is all about.

TWO TYPES OF URGENCY

When we think about urgency, we typically think about what the customer will be missing out on if he or she doesn't move forward today. Advertisers have a field day with this type of thinking:

- "One at this price"
- "While supplies last"
- "Offer good through …"

This type of urgency is designed to get people off the fence. Here's the key question: What got them on the fence in the first place? The answer: dissatisfaction!

The fact is that there are two distinct types of buyer urgency:

1. Circumstantial urgency
2. Personal urgency

Circumstantial urgency is about what the customer will miss out on if he doesn't move forward today. When we think about discounts that are available for a limited time only, or special below-market financing, or a low amount of available stock, all those things speak to circumstantial urgency.

Personal urgency is about why the customer is in your sales center in the first place. It's about what's wrong with her life and what needs to change. It is centered on dissatisfaction and the desire to improve her current situation.

Circumstantial Urgency	Personal Urgency
• What they miss out on if they don't buy	• Why they need to buy in the first place
• Motivated by promotions	• Motivated by dissatisfaction
• Will buy when the deal is right	• Will buy when the CD is high
• "One at this price"	• "Improve your life"

Which is more important: circumstantial urgency or personal urgency? I would contend that in the absence of personal urgency, we find that circumstantial urgency is rendered irrelevant.

For example, have you ever looked at items for sale on a deep discount rack? I mean the *deep* discount rack, like the clearance rack in the back of an outlet store, where everything is "now 80 percent off!" What kind of clothes make it to the clearance rack in an outlet store, for crying out loud? Are they a great deal? You betcha. Have you ever bought everything that's on such a rack? Probably not, especially if you had no need (personal urgency) for the clothes in the first place. But if you forgot to pack a black dress belt . . . .

IT'S ALL ABOUT THE CD

You've probably been in a situation where you found yourself at a Level 10 dissatisfaction.

- Your car died unexpectedly.
- You got a sudden and unexpected job transfer, and you needed a place to live immediately.
- Your extremely full refrigerator stopped working the day before you were to host Thanksgiving for the extended family.
- Your luggage was lost on day one of your vacation, and you needed something to wear.

> *If there is dissatisfaction with the status quo, good. If there is ferment, so much the better. If there is restlessness, I am pleased. Then let there be ideas, and hard thought, and hard work. If man feels small, let man make himself bigger.*
>
> —HUBERT H. HUMPHREY

In each of these cases—and countless others—the price and the product were not the key factors in your purchase decision. The sale was based on a Current Dissatisfaction, and the CD created the urgency. But note that the CD also created the discomfort. When we desire to escape discomfort of a certain level, then we are practically forced to take action.

I want to challenge you to consider how important this conversation is as it relates to your own sales presentation. Think of your typical sales encounter and ask yourself how early in the conversation the "why" question appears. Many sales discussions are about the product or the terms or the deal, but personal urgency is the prospect's primary motivation for being there in the first place. Therefore, it only makes sense that the question of why a prospect is dissatisfied should be the starting point in every sales conversation.

Put another way, most sales presentations are focused on what the customer is moving *to*. The best salespeople on the planet first focus on what the customer is moving *from*.

ANYONE NEED A MATTRESS?

I have this weird fantasy about working in a mattress store for a weekend. I know this might sound arrogant, but if I were selling mattresses, I would clean up. I would predict about a 90 percent conversion rate for everyone who walked into my mattress store. Let me tell you my secret.

In a typical mattress store experience, the salesperson will open with something like, "Can I help you?" This is, of course, a "script of life" question that one typically hears from a salesperson, and typical customers have their scripted answer already prepared: "We're just looking."

Uh . . . no, they're not. I'm sorry, but there is no way that a customer in a mattress store is "just looking." Everyone who darkens the doorway of a mattress store has a problem. Think about it; when was the last time you walked into a mattress store for kicks, just because you were curious about the latest and greatest mattress innovations, even though you were perfectly happy in your current situation? Not gonna happen. You are in the store because you have a problem, and it is in this Current Dissatisfaction that we find the path to the sale.

Yet how many sales presentations start with either a discussion of the mattress selection and product information, or price and a discussion of the current sales promotion? Now consider the various reasons that people buy mattresses:

- Their youngest child is graduating from a crib.
- They just moved—they now have a guest room.
- They're just married—they need something for two.
- She's just divorced—she needs something for one.
- His doctor said, "Upgrade today or get back surgery in five years."
- I just came into money—it's time to take care of myself.
- She's bleeding in the right thigh from a spring that has popped out.

Look at that list. In every case, it is the desire to improve his or her life (CD) that motivates the customer. A great product is the solution and the terms are the enabler, but the CD is what brought the customer to the store. It is a problem that must be solved (and I'll clean up in my mattress-selling efforts by doing so, thank you!).

EMOTIONAL DISSATISFACTION

Until you know how the current dissatisfaction affects the customer on an emotional level, your understanding is incomplete.

One last consideration as it relates to CD: until you know how the CD affects the customer on an emotional level, your understanding is incomplete. People don't purchase because of their CD; they purchase because of how they feel about their CD. Their CD brings about frustration, and frustration causes action. This is where that strong discomfort forces our hand.

I remember a new home sales representative telling me about a man who came into her sales center suggesting that his home was too small. This was true, but it was hardly enough of a backstory to let the salesperson understand the emotional aspects of the customer's dissatisfaction.

Further probing led to the discovery that the home had been built 80 years ago, a time when one bathroom somehow seemed sufficient. Again, that's interesting, but it is not yet compelling. Until we discover how this affects the customer emotionally, we are underequipped to solve his problem.

Upon probing further, the salesperson learned that this man had three daughters, ages 10, 12, and 15. Hold the phone! Excuse me? Three girls *and* his wife are all sharing the same bathroom? Stop and imagine what that would be like. What are the mornings like when all three girls are getting ready for school? And where does this guy shower—at the YMCA?

This man was in the market to buy a home, and he told the sales representative that he was interested in something with at least two bathrooms. But what was he really buying? I'll tell you something—it wasn't bathroom count! He was buying peace in his household. He was buying better relationships for his family. He was buying a happy home.

Consider the customer who senses that she is underinsured. She tells her agent that she wants to increase her life insurance policy, but what is she really doing? Is it truly a financial move? I would argue that the product is not insurance, but rather peace of mind—a good night's sleep. She is making a move to alleviate the nagging feeling that she is not providing for the care of her family the way she should. She is buying a sense of doing the right thing. That is emotional reasoning, not financial reasoning.

Think about taking a deeper dive into your own habits of sales questioning. Until you understand the discomfort that a customer is enduring in any given situation, you are underequipped to sell that customer anything at all. Even a simple query, like "tell me more about that," can go a long way toward understanding the emotional aspects of the customer's CD.

BOLDNESS IN QUESTIONING

Always the beautiful answer who asks a more beautiful question.

—e. e. CUMMINGS

I'll close this chapter with both a concern and a challenge.

Here's the problem: understanding the CD on an emotional level takes a level of questioning that is deeper than many salespeople are comfortable with (there's that word again!). Deep discovery requires a degree of boldness in questioning, and many salespeople simply cannot handle this fact.

Because of the salesperson's discomfort, there is a default to the easier questions. The problem is that while the typical questions are easier to ask, they simply don't get us anywhere.

Consider the following sales questions:

- "Can I help you?"
- "Have you been here before?"
- "What are you looking for?"
- "Do you have any questions?"

All of these are easy questions to ask, but what are the odds that you'll understand the customer's pain points when you ask this level of questions?

Suppose you're selling motorcycles and a man comes in and starts looking around. He doesn't look like an experienced rider; in fact, he seems somewhat perplexed. The conversation might sound something like this:

SALESPERSON: "Can I help you?"

CUSTOMER: "I'm just looking around."

SALESPERSON: "OK. Anything specific you're looking for?"

CUSTOMER: "Well, I guess something that's easy to handle."

SALESPERSON: "Do you have a price range in mind?"

CUSTOMER: "I'd like to keep it under $8,000."

SALESPERSON: "Okay. I have three different bikes I can show you."

Let's evaluate. Remember that there are two types of salespeople: "from" salespeople and "to" salespeople. Is this salesperson more interested in what the customer is coming from or in what the customer is moving to? The answer is obvious; he is a *to* salesperson, and in no time at all we will observe a feature-dumping sales presentation followed by a discussion of our end-of-the-month blowout extravaganza.

Has the salesperson done anything at all to understand the customer's discomfort, let alone alleviate that discomfort? No, nothing.

Let's see how the bold sales professional might handle this same scenario.

SALESPERSON: "Good afternoon. How are you doing today?"

CUSTOMER: "Fine, thanks."

SALESPERSON: "So you're looking around at motorcycles. Do you ride now, or are you thinking about joining the club?"

CUSTOMER: "I've been thinking about it for a while now."

SALESPERSON: "That's awesome. You're in for a thrill. I'll help in any way I can. Can I ask you a couple of quick questions just so I can point you in the right direction?"

CUSTOMER: "Sure."

SALESPERSON: "Let's start here. Tell me what got you thinking that it might be time to buy a motorcycle."

CUSTOMER: "Oh, . . . well, . . . I'm kinda on my own suddenly and I've always wanted to ride a bike, but it just didn't work out before."

SALESPERSON: "Got it. It's a new season in life, and you are looking to do what you've always wanted to do."

CUSTOMER: "Always wanted to do, but she never let me do."

SALESPERSON: "I certainly understand. When you think about riding a motorcycle, give me the mental image. Is it a long trip across several states? Racing forward on a green light? Or just cruising down a winding road? What are you thinking?"

I'll stop here, but do you see the progression? The bold salesperson is connecting on a level that the timid salesperson will never get to, and the bond of trust that has now been established will make the demonstration far more effective. This sale has already been made; now it's just about figuring out the details.

Ask any successful salesperson and she'll tell you the same thing: she doesn't rest until she understands the deeper pain. She needs to understand the customer's objective on an emotional level. She is a from salesperson before she becomes a to salesperson.

Challenge yourself: how much do you *need* to know? How can you increase your boldness in the simple questions up front in order to learn things that your competitors will never discover?

A STARTING POINT: "TELL ME MORE . . ."

Let me make a suggestion to help you get started on the path of deeper discovery. Get used to the phrase "tell me more." I recommend that you get into the habit of digging deeper in your daily interactions with your kids, your spouse, the barista at Starbucks, or anyone else that you meet. This isn't just a great sales skill—it's a great life skill. It is also the ticket to understanding your customers on a new and deeper level.

Curiosity is one of the most underdeveloped and underappreciated traits of great salespeople. If you can build that curiosity muscle, you can discover things about people that no one else is likely to figure out.

I have no special talent. I am only passionately curious.

—ALBERT EINSTEIN

Questions to Ponder

- On a scale of 1 to 10, rate your current level of dissatisfaction with the car you are driving right now. Compare your dissatisfaction today with your dissatisfaction on the day you took ownership of the car—is it higher or lower today? What level of dissatisfaction will you have to reach before you buy a new car?

- What is the relationship between dissatisfaction and discomfort? As a sales professional who is pursuing boldness, how does this inform your relationship with and your duties to your customers?

- What is the difference between circumstantial urgency and personal urgency? Reflect on your own sales presentation: Is it more often tied to circumstantial urgency or to personal urgency? Which form of urgency is more powerful in the prospect's decision-making process? What are some ways in which you can better tailor your sales presentation to personal urgency?

- Are the words "tell me more about that" a regular part of your vocabulary right now? If you were to incorporate that phrase into more of your sales presentations, how would it change your understanding of your customer? If you were to incorporate that phrase into more of your personal conversations, how would it change your relationships?

Now Try This . . .

Take a few minutes to brainstorm 10 variations of the phrase "tell me more about that" to incorporate into your sales presentation. Use different words, and use language that you are comfortable delivering to a customer, but make sure you stick to the concept of digging deeper:

1. _____

2. _____

3. _____

4. _____

5. _____

6. _____

7. _____

8. _____

9. _____

10. _____

The Customer's Mission
Future Promise

The aim of marketing is to know and understand the customer so well the product or service fits him and sells itself.

—Peter Drucker

THE BIG IDEA
The most effective sales presentation offers an emotion-based Future Promise as a solution to an emotion-based Current Dissatisfaction.

DEFINING THE FUTURE PROMISE

If prospects are to become owners, they must deal with their own internal issues in order to overcome their discomfort. We've just discussed the Current Dissatisfaction (CD), the motivating force that gets a potential customer off the sofa and into active shopping mode. As I have suggested, the CD is what the prospect is moving from; now let's talk about what that prospect is moving to.

It is important to understand that if there is a compelling Current Dissatisfaction, there must also be a compelling Future Promise (FP). The FP is that magical place in the customer's mind where his mission is fulfilled. It represents the best possible outcome of his search. That doesn't mean that the solution is perfect, but rather that the solution solves the problem and does so in a way that exceeds the value equation offered by any competitor.

By way of definition, the word *promise* in Future Promise is not something I am promising to my customer. Rather, it is her own perceived promise of an improved life. You could use the word *hope* here, as in the hope of things to come.

The FP is shiny and new. It induces feelings of future pride and of joy. The FP offers a sense of what life could look like, a stark contrast to the discomfort of the CD. In many ways, the FP is the opposite of discomfort.

Consider a soon-to-be-retired couple who are shopping for their first recreational vehicle. Up to this point in their lives, their vacations have consisted of getting on a plane and cramming as many activities as possible into a two-week timeframe. They are through with that type of vacation, as they are now finding that it leaves them more tired when they return than they were when they left. Their dissatisfaction with their vacation lifestyle has taken its toll.

This couple may not know exactly what features they want in their new motor home. In fact, they are likely to be extremely fuzzy about the options and somewhat intimidated by their lack of knowledge about the details. They only know that they have friends who have sold them on the idea of the RV lifestyle. They have only a vague vision of their future life.

The RV itself represents that life. This isn't about the product, but rather about the promise. It's not about the features; it's about what the features mean for their future enjoyment. Any salesperson who tries to overwhelm them with details about the RV's features without understanding the psychological nature of the purchase decision is doomed to fail. This is the precise reason why feature dumping will destroy both the relationship and the sale. A top professional will not sell the customer a recreational vehicle; she will sell the way the customer will *feel* when he is using a recreational vehicle.

Or, consider designer shoes. You're walking through the mall, and you see these shoes. They are *way* out of your price range, but they are stunningly beautiful. You start thinking about how you will feel when you're wearing them, and how your friends will "ooh" and "ahh." You think about how they will perfectly complement your latest new outfit. You feel that you and this pair of shoes were "meant to be."

> *The Future Promise is about the mental picture that we create, one of extreme pleasure and satisfaction in a newly improved life.*

May I point out that this discussion has nothing to do with the features of the shoes? The FP is about the mental picture that we create, one of extreme pleasure and satisfaction in our newly improved life. Consequently, when it comes to sales, a low FP is disastrous, but a high FP is not merely compelling, it takes on a kismet quality for many customers.

THE FUTURE PROMISE SCALE

As is the case with the CD, we can put the FP on a scale. As a prospect considers her options, she will subconsciously value the offering, weighing the FP against other factors.

- A weight of 1 to 3 means that she's just not that into the product.
- A weight of 4 to 6 suggests an interest level, but not high enough to lead to a purchase.
- A weight of 7 to 9 indicates a very serious leaning toward purchasing.
- A weight of 10 says, "I have to have that, and I have to have it now!"

As is the case with the CD, the higher the FP rating, the likelier the purchase. We've all been in a situation where we just had to have something. The emotional pull of the FP can at times be irresistibly strong.

On our tenth anniversary, Karen and I were in beautiful Carmel, California. We stumbled upon an antique store, and we instantly fell in love with an eighteenth-century French armoire. It was stunning, and we knew that if we decided to buy it, this armoire would be the most expensive piece of furniture in our home.

I need to point out that this was not in our budget (and, in fact, that our budget was nonexistent at the time). We had no compelling need for it; we did not have a significant storage problem. But the armoire represented a dramatic Future Promise, and so we bought it. Retailers call this "impulse buying." I call it a "10 FP."

In the absence of a CD, the FP can stand alone as a compelling motivating factor; in fact, a majority of salespeople get by with hoping that the FP alone will carry the sale. Sometimes they are correct in that assessment, but it is a strategy that is based principally on hope.

But imagine that on top of our passion for the armoire we also had a significant need. That would change everything.

THE CURRENT DISSATISFACTION– FUTURE PROMISE CONNECTION

Typically, the FP serves as a countering force to the CD:

- I'm hungry—the sandwich looks good.
- I have no jewelry for this outfit—these earrings are perfect.
- My portfolio is not diversified—this mutual fund is attractive.
- My complexion is bad—this moisturizer will help.

Suppose a home shopper has had it with her outdated kitchen; she has a high CD. She visits a model show home and sees her dream kitchen; it becomes her FP.

Consider a young couple looking at a high-end surround sound stereo system. Their current sound system is dated and even embarrassing; they have a high CD. They see a state-of-the-art system that they believe will deliver everything they are looking for; that's their FP.

It is important to note that the CD and the FP are sequential. While the FP certainly can stand alone (remember the armoire), it is most effective as a response to a compelling CD.

Too many presentations start with the FP discussion and never accurately assess the CD. And while it is possible to get the sale using this method, you can bank on coming up short of your true sales potential until you really understand the CD, and understand it early in the process.

Consider the sales of fractional vacation ownership (timeshares, if you will). For those of you who have been to a presentation of such a product (and who hasn't?), what do the promoters talk about first? Note that the good ones do not lead with the product (FP), they lead with the problem (CD).

Effective vacation ownership salespeople ask you about what you do now on your vacations. They discuss your vacation habits—what has worked well and what has not. Ultimately, they will point out that your current method of planning your vacations might not be in your long-term best interest. *Then* they share the FP. Your dissatisfaction might have been low coming in, but it is raging now.

Let me remind you that the problem we face is dealing with your customer's discomfort. If the dissatisfaction is based on emotion (fear, disgust, or embarrassment), then you cannot counter that emotional discomfort with a feature. Put simply, the most effective sales presentations always present the FP as an exciting solution to an emotion-based dissatisfaction. Does yours?

THE VAGUE FP

*As for the future, your task is not to foresee it,
but to enable it.*

—Antoine de Saint-Exupéry

For many customers, the CD is not particularly well defined, at least not initially. They come in with comments like, "We're just looking around," or, "We just want to browse," or my favorite, "We'll know it when we see it."

Show of hands, please, if you hate the line, "We'll know it when we see it." I hate to break it to you, but I'm the guy who says that! I am the guy who is likely to say, "I'll know it when I see it."

Now I'm going to let you into our little club. I'm going to divulge the secret meaning of those of us who regularly say, "I'll know it when I see it." I'm violating the rules here, so pay attention.

What I really mean is ... (wait for it) ... I'll know it when I see it!

Seriously, I'm not trying to put you off. I am a visual buyer, and either things speak to me or they don't. I often cannot describe what I am looking for, but when I see it, I act. If you want to know my FP, it would be very wise of you to determine what I have been attracted to in the past.

As I write this, my wife and I are in the process of a major redecoration effort. We purchased a home in a great location, but the interior was badly dated (the pink oval tub with columns on each side is a giveaway). While we have a difficult time describing what we like, we know it when we see it. Our interior decorator offered us some excellent advice: go on houzz.com and save all the photos that you like to your favorites page (houzz.com is sort of a Pinterest for homes). We can see trends by identifying those visual preferences.

Don't be dismayed by people who have a vague FP. Give them a similar assignment, and it might equip you to understand what they cannot tell you themselves.

HOW THE FUTURE PROMISE CAN CREATE A CURRENT DISSATISFACTION

We've talked about how the CD and the FP blend. Now let's talk about a really cool extension of what we've learned so far. This is the fun part if you get it right.

Here's what happens: a compelling FP can literally create a CD out of nothing.

Let's suppose your best friend buys a new car and wants to take you out to lunch to celebrate. Of course, she will drive. You meet up somewhere, and you get out of your perfectly satisfactory car and into her brand-new car. As you get in, you notice several cool things:

- That wonderful new car smell
- The push-button ignition that works while the key stays in her purse
- The backup camera on the dashboard
- The air-conditioned seats

After lunch, your friend drops you off, and you get back into your old car. Now what happens?

- You take a big whiff and ask, "What is that smell?"
- You have to fumble for your keys in your purse.
- You have to crank your head to look behind you when you're backing up.
- Your seat is blistering hot.

Before you sat in your friend's brand-new car, you were perfectly happy with your car. Where are you now? Pointed in the direction of a car dealership!

Don't be dismayed by people who seem to have a low CD during the early discovery period. Sometimes a customer needs to see a strong FP in order to create a CD.

ELEVATING THE CD DURING THE DEMONSTRATION PROCESS

Here's a technique that can help you pump up that CD during the product demonstration. When you are demonstrating your product and you see your customer's eyes light up, immediately ask him about his CD.

- "How does this compare to what you have now?"
- "Do you have anything like this now?"
- "What are you doing now, since you don't have this?"

This is a double scoop of sales success. You assess the customer's perceived value of the compelling Future Promise in what you are sharing, and at the same time, you pump up the customer's Current Dissatisfaction with what he has now. It's a twofer!

Remember the greater context of our discussion. This portion of the book deals with the buyer's discomfort levels. Change carries inherent discomfort, and buying a product means change. We must provide both a maximum CD and a correspondingly high FP if we are to move this customer through the pain of change and forward toward a purchase.

EMOTIONAL PROMISE

Like the CD, the FP has been truly discovered only when it can be expressed in emotional terms. A woman doesn't buy the necklace; she buys how she feels when she is wearing the necklace. A man doesn't buy the computer; he buys a sense of excitement in his increased productivity and enjoyment. People don't buy the boat; they buy the laughter and exhilaration of being on the lake.

> *People don't buy products. They buy the solutions that the products represent.*
>
> —NIDO QUBEIN

This is a major problem with many sales presentations, and I'm sure you've witnessed this yourself as a consumer. I see salespeople all the time who display all the passion and flair of an IRS agent during a corporate audit. Here's a tip: if you are in any way excited about the product you are selling . . . be sure to let your face show it.

We literally rob the customer of the opportunity to get emotionally involved when we ourselves are dispassionate about what we represent. After all, if we are not excited about the product we are selling, how can we expect customers to be excited?

Both my daughter and my daughter-in-law sell Mary Kay cosmetics. When the family is together, I am bound to hear (in *very* excited tones) about this absolutely amazing moisturizer or that incredibly effective cover-up. Based on their enthusiasm alone, I am fairly certain that these products will cure cancer! Their enthusiasm is the Mary Kay equivalent of when the camera turns to the guys in the front row at a football game. It would not surprise me in any way to hear my girls yelling, "Yeah! Mary Kay rocks! Whoo-hoo! Number one, babeeee!"

Nothing in that description is a criticism. On the contrary, consider the potential for success of a Mary Kay consultant who is shy, mousy, and bland. It doesn't work. Customers do not simply purchase the product; they also purchase the seller's enthusiasm. The demonstrable emotion of a salesperson who is truly excited about his or her product is adopted by the customer, and that makes the purchase process more enjoyable. If your customer cannot engage with you emotionally, you've got a serious problem.

POTENTIAL FUTURE PROMISE POINTS

The Future Promise is best applied when it is tailored specifically for the prospect in front of you. That said, it would be in your best interest to really think through the potential FP points of your product offering in advance. You probably already know what many of them are (you'll find a list in your product brochure); now you need to express them in emotional terms.

When you establish trust with your customer, you can ask questions that will cause him to express his FP in a manner that demonstrates emotional connection:

- "Give me a sense of how you will feel tomorrow morning after you have upgraded your life insurance this afternoon."

- "Tell me what your mental state will be when you're out on the road in this RV."
- "Whom will you tell first that you bought this big-screen TV?"
- "Put yourself in front of the mirror getting ready to go out this Friday night. How do you feel?"

Fair warning on this. Remember our discussions on being "coffee-worthy" to your customer? Being coffee-worthy implies that you are not looking for your new best friend, but rather that your customer will quickly say, "Yeah, I'd have a cup of coffee with that person."

That established relational bond is a critical precursor to asking these emotion-based questions effectively. If you sound like a typical salesperson, those questions will seem nosy and manipulative, and they will actually serve to destroy trust. But if the trust has already been established and you really are interested in the answers, these questions will take you to levels that most salespeople can only dream about.

Remember that in the absence of an emotional FP, your chances of landing the sale are slim. Your task is to help customers clarify their own emotions surrounding the FP.

THE SECRET OF AN EFFECTIVE DEMONSTRATION

The demonstration is not about the product—it's about the customer.

One last perspective before we move on. One of the most common mistakes in sales is thinking that the demonstration is about the product. I assure you that it is not.

Be clear on this: the demonstration is not about the product—it's about the customer.

Too many demonstrations are focused on features: this does this and that does that. The more advanced version of the demonstration includes not only the features, but also the benefits. (You remember this from your sales training, right?)

But the *most* effective demonstrations are about neither features nor benefits, but rather about helping the customers to carry out their mission—the mission to improve their lives. An effective presentation incorporates a theme that communicates: "You said this, so let me show you that." "You said you were frustrated by this, so let me show you that."

Stay customer-centered in your demonstration and you'll improve your technique dramatically.

Questions to Ponder

- Think of a dissatisfaction in your life right now—your home, your car, your smartphone, or whatever is relevant for you. Now take a moment to think about the corollary Future Promise: what do you "see" for yourself once you've solved the dissatisfaction? How will you feel? How will your life improve?

- Which is more powerful: presenting the *features* of a Future Promise or focusing on the *emotions* of a Future Promise? What are some techniques you can adopt to speak to your customer's emotions instead of merely talking about the features of your product?

- Do you see a link here between your own boldness level and your ability to deal with your customers on an emotional level? What are some areas of discomfort that you personally face when you think about digging deeper into your customer's emotional state of mind?

- What does this statement mean to you: "*The demonstration is not about the product—it's about the customer*"? Are you ever guilty of making your demonstrations about the product instead of the customer? What does that look like? What would a customer-centered demonstration look like?

Now Try This . . .

Think of a prospect you're currently working with or a customer who recently purchased. Using the table below, map out the customer's Current Dissatisfaction and Future Promise, then "fill in the gaps" with descriptive language about the emotions associated with each.

Take time to complete this exercise thoroughly, as it will lay the foundation for the remaining two chapters of the book.

Current Dissatisfaction	Emotions They Currently Feel	Future Promise	Emotions They Want to Feel

The Customer's Mission
Cost and Fear

*Twenty years from now you will be more disappointed by
the things that you didn't do than by the ones you did do.
So throw off the bowlines. Sail away from the safe harbor.
Catch the trade winds in your sails. Explore. Dream. Discover.*

—Mark Twain

THE BIG IDEA
*Cost and Fear are the discomforts that the prospect
must overcome in order to make a purchase decision.*

THE SALES INHIBITORS

In her classic book *Feel the Fear and Do It Anyway*, the late Dr. Susan Jeffers points out that fear is a mental process, and that it is a problem only if we give in to the idea that we are out of control. Her mantra of "I can handle it!" speaks to the sense of self-determination that we have at our disposal should we choose to accept it.

Jeffers writes, "If everybody feels the fear when approaching something new in life, yet so many are out there 'doing it' despite the fear, then we must conclude that fear is not the problem. Obviously. The real issue has nothing to do with the fear itself, but rather how we hold the fear."

Current Dissatisfaction and Future Promise are motivating factors. They propel the customer forward toward a purchase decision. At the same time, there are competing factors that are holding your customers back. Any purchase decision requires that a prospect overcome certain discomforts; those discomforts are found in these inhibiting factors.

I call these factors Cost and Fear, or Cost/Fear (C/F). Consider Cost/Fear to be the barriers or hurdles over which the prospect must jump. They might be relatively low (the price of a pack of gum) or sky-high (the fear in buying a new home). In any event, the C/F must be addressed if we are to earn more sales.

> *Understanding the Cost and Fear is critical because this is where the customer's paralyzing discomfort is found.*

Understanding the C/F is critical because this is where the customer's paralyzing discomfort is found. Remember that at any given time, there are two sets of discomforts at play: yours and your customers'. Further understand that your customers are fighting their own internal discomfort war. On one side is the Current Dissatisfaction; on the other is the Cost/Fear involved in acting upon that dissatisfaction.

Our task is to get them beyond their Cost/Fear discomfort.

A TALE OF TWO SUITS

There are a number of ways to accomplish this objective, and they can have varying degrees of success. Several months back, my wife came to me to announce that Macy's was having a one-day sale. If you've spent any time at Macy's, you already know that this is hardly a rare event. Macy's holds one-day sales seemingly every week. Oddly enough, its "one-day sales" tend to start on Friday and end on Sunday (I still haven't figured that one out).

But this was not just any one-day sale. Karen was waving a "Preferred Customer" coupon that was available for use on a Friday morning before 11:00 a.m. Now, I know what you're thinking: "Just when I thought I could not be more impressed with Jeff Shore, now I learn that he is a Macy's preferred customer!" And really, how many can there be?

We traipsed down to the Roseville Galleria and entered the mall. Karen headed to the women's department, and I decided to browse the suit selection. With my coupons and their discounts, I was prepared to find the deal of a lifetime. ("With all your discounts and coupons the total comes to . . . well how about that—we owe you 12 dollars.")

After looking around and trying on several items, it came down to a decision between two suits. In my right hand, I was holding a very nice Hugo Boss suit. I loved it. It was solid black and had great lines, and if I'm going to be perfectly blunt, I think I looked good in it. Here's the problem: the suit cost $700, which is more than I'm used to spending for a suit. And it wasn't on sale.

In my left hand, I was holding a different suit. I don't remember the brand name; I just remember that I liked it. I didn't love it the way I loved the Hugo Boss, but it was a great sale: normally $550 and now $250. I mean, how do you beat that?

Which suit do you think I purchased? It should be obvious to you from the circumstances. Question: when my hand hit the door at Macy's, what one word was screaming through my brain? That word was "*deal*," and until a sales professional could take me off that mental path, I was not going to pay full price for anything. Macy's has, over the years, literally trained me to never pay full price for anything in the store.

So there I was with my newly purchased suit, but Karen still had more shopping to do. I was shopped out. One suit—that's about my shopping limit. I wandered to the other end of the mall and entered a Nordstrom. I wasn't there to buy anything; this was simply "shoppertainment."

I was browsing the Nordstrom brand dress shirts just to look at the styles. I have purchased a good number of those shirts in the past, but I had no intention of purchasing any that day—that is, until a young lady approached me and strung together the only words in the English language that could get me to consider buying something right then.

"I think you should be looking at the trim-cut shirts," she said.

"Excuse me?" I said, suddenly feeling the need to stand up tall and puff my chest out just a bit.

"You need a tailored shirt that tapers in for your thinner waist. The shirts you are looking at here are not tailored, so you'll end up with a lot of material coming out of the back of your trousers. Most men can't wear the trim-cut shirts, but you definitely can."

"Yes . . . um . . . of course. That's right! I was just shopping . . . um . . . for a friend. Tell me, where are these magical shirts?"

I guess I got carried away; I really wasn't paying much attention. The next thing I knew, that young lady was sliding a charge slip across the counter at me and I had just spent $550 on dress shirts!

Let's analyze this. Macy's was all about lowering the Cost in order to induce me to buy, and consequently I ended up undervaluing the product. The Nordstrom representative played on both my Current Dissatisfaction and my Future Promise. The Future Promise was all about looking better in a slimmer shirt. The Current Dissatisfaction was based on the fact that every shirt in my closet was now deficient.

COST DEFINED

> *If you do not first understand the customer's Current Dissatisfaction and Future Promise, you will be left to compete on Cost alone.*

That story suggests something very important. If you do not first understand the customer's CD and FP, you will be left to compete on cost alone. In that case, my friend, I hope you are planning on very deep discounts, because that is the only way to win the C/F game. You will have been reduced to a commodity, nothing more.

To be clear on the terms used here, "Cost" relates to any price to be paid, whether it be financial, emotional, inconvenience, time investment, or something else. The natural first thought here is "price" (or, in many cases, "payment"). Of course, the monetary amount is an important component of Cost, but we cannot stop there—it's not even close.

There are often ancillary financial costs in addition to the primary cost. If I buy an expensive ring, I might have to insure it. New skis require a new rack on my car. Buying an RV might also mean buying an enclosure for it.

Then we consider the cost of change. Many people simply don't like change—any change. For many, change is inherently negative because it means moving out of and away from a current comfort level. Because of this, consider just how much mental energy goes into a purchase decision for people who strongly dislike and usually avoid change. (They are already worn out from merely considering a change before they even get to you!)

Now consider the hassle factor. It's a pain to go through the process of identifying a new car, visiting dealerships, sitting down in the finance manager's office, and so on. The initial emotion wears off, and all that remains is hassle (which explains why customers get grumpy).

Many sales professionals make the mistake of spending too little time discussing cost. They want to avoid any discussion that could be painful, so they slip it under the rug. I disagree with this approach. The cost concerns are there, whether you are up front about them or not. If you want to be a trusted advisor, you need to address cost boldly. Ultimately, evading the issue of cost is disrespectful to your customers and damaging to your relationship with them.

FEAR DEFINED

Accompanying the Cost concern is the issue of a prospect's many Fears. Fear is often a debilitating issue for would-be customers. Fear can be tied to any number of things:

- *Fear of commitment.* Concern over whether this is a wise decision.
- *Fear of making the wrong choice.* There are so many options out there; how do we know which is best?
- *Fear of the financial obligation.* This is especially true for big-ticket purchases.
- *Fear of what other people will think.* Peer pressure is a powerful motivating force.
- *Fear of overpaying.* Is the value really there?
- *Fear of buying at the wrong time.* Does this make sense for me today?

> I learned that courage was not the absence of fear, but the triumph over it. The brave man is not he who does not feel afraid, but he who conquers that fear.
>
> —NELSON MANDELA

There are many more such fears, all of them real and significant. These fears reside in a prospect's emotions and must be dealt with in order to move a customer forward. To ignore these very real fears is to leave the customer to deal with discomforts on his own. And more often than not, doing that means losing a sale. Fear is a powerful motivator of *in*action; a customer who is overwhelmed by his unspoken fears will act quickly to escape the feeling of being overwhelmed. Almost always, that action will be not buying rather than making a purchase.

RATING THE COST/FEAR

Just like a prospect's CD and FP, her C/F can also be placed on a scale. In this case, of course, the lower the score, the better when it comes to moving forward with a purchase decision.

In light of the C/F scale, let's tackle an uncomfortable truth head-on. Show me a prospect with a 10 C/F, and I'll show you a nonprospect. A very high C/F indicates that the cost and/or the fear are so high that a purchase decision is simply not possible.

In a glaringly obvious example, a prospect might be very interested in a Porsche 911, but have no money and no job. The acquisition is impossible for financial reasons—that is a Level 10 C/F. Or a customer might really want a hot tub, but he tells you that he lives in an apartment building that forbids such things. The C/F is a 10. These people are nonbuyers.

Of course, the lower the C/F, the easier the purchase decision. This explains the discount retailer's approach of offering huge deals. ("Today only! Take an additional 25 percent off clearance prices!") Theoretically, if the price is low enough, we will purchase a discounted item even if we are not in love with it.

Think about that for a moment. May I have a show of hands of everyone out there who has owned a piece of clothing for 30 days or more that still has the price tag on it? Next question: did you get that item on sale? In all probability, you did. Things we pay full price for, we wear right away. But that item you picked up off the clearance rack had such a seemingly low C/F threshold that you simply could not pass it up. (Unfortunately, the FP was also low; we'll get back to that.)

The (All-Too) Typical Approach

We tend to think that buyers are concerned only about price. I believe this belief comes about because of our desire to escape the discomfort of a price challenge. We simply do not like price objections. They are uncomfortable. And so we counter a potential objection with a proactive price discount. Our "story" at this point is that we are simply removing barriers to the sale.

Unfortunately, the net effect of this approach is that we are, in reality, buying off our customers. The message is as follows: "I believe I can discount this product so much that you won't have a choice, even if you are not truly in love with it."

Conversely, think of an item of clothing in your closet right now that you absolutely love. Now ask yourself: did you pay full price for it? You probably did. And if you paid full price for it, how soon after you bought it did you first wear it? Hmm.

Preemptive discounting causes a customer to look askance at your product. The instinctive reaction to a lowered price tends to be, "What's wrong with it?" As Thomas Paine famously said, "What we obtain too cheap, we esteem too lightly."

What About "the Event"?

Have you noticed in recent years that car dealerships rarely have "sales" anymore? Every commercial speaks of an "event": "Hurry down to your Ford dealer for our Summer Savings Event!" Car sellers are on to the fact that customers have grown weary of and skeptical about the constant barrage of sales messages. People can see and hear about "A great sale!" only so many times before skepticism turns into apathy. What word do you think will soon replace *event*?

> *When you lead off by lowering the Cost and Fear barrier, the product itself is going to take a value perception hit.*

Is there room for a good old-fashioned "sale"? Of course there is. Just understand that when you lead off by lowering the C/F barrier, the product itself is going to take a value perception hit.

Much of my career has been spent in the home selling business. I have seen markets come and go, with huge fluctuations along the way. I remember driving down Highway 65 in Lincoln, California, in 2008 when I saw a home builder's billboard with a sign rider that said, "Incentives up to $200,000."

Excuse me? A $200,000 incentive? You read that right. Question: How strong was the sales pace at this new home community? Answer: It was dead in the water. After a while, discounting is nothing but white noise.

Conversely, in 2013, in a rebounding market, I heard from countless new home salespeople that prices were going up fast. But at the same time, I saw price sheets in the sales offices for those same new homes offering $7,500 closing cost credits. Why? How do you raise prices on the one hand and discount on the other without thoroughly confusing your value equation?

My opinion is that the discount itself becomes a drug for the buyer . . . and the seller. It becomes a part of the culture that is very difficult to undo (just ask JC Penney!). Once the expectation of a discount is fully rooted in a specific buying culture, we have to offer a discount in order to make a sale.

Or do we? Ask Nordstrom. Or CarMax. Or In-N-Out Burger. Or the Shane Company. In these places, sales and coupons are almost nonexistent. They exist on value alone.

Can you attract business by offering a discount? Yes, you can. Just understand that the customer will perceive the discount as applying not only to the price, but also to the product itself.

Questions to Ponder

- Can you think of a time in your life when Cost and Fear held you back from making a decision, even when you had a strong Current Dissatisfaction and a compelling Future Promise? What factors would have had to change in order for you to make that decision?

- What happens if you do not understand your customer's Cost and Fear on an emotional level? What are the drawbacks of competing on price alone? How will boldness enable you to deal more directly with the customer's emotional sense of Cost and Fear?

- Why can a discounted price (lower Cost) actually wind up creating a lower Future Promise for your customer? In your experience, which customers are ultimately tougher to satisfy—those who are motivated by price alone, or those who feel an emotional connection to the product?

- Do you face any selling discomforts that cause you to focus on price rather than on understanding and meeting the customer's emotional needs? What paradigm shifts might this require for you? What decisions for boldness must you make? What new stories can you begin telling yourself to enable new choices and new behaviors?

Now Try This . . .

Look back at the table you completed at the end of Chapter 14. Once again, write down this customer's Current Dissatisfaction and Future Promise in the table below.

Next, complete your analysis by identifying the Costs and Fears that are currently holding this customer back. Then take a deeper dive and write down some of the emotional hurdles that this customer will need to overcome in order to minimize the Cost and Fear inhibitors.

Be thorough in your answers—we'll put all of this together in the next chapter to help you move your customer toward a purchase decision that will change his world!

Current Dissatisfaction	Future Promise	Costs and Fears	Emotional Hurdles to Overcome

Putting It All Together
The Buying Formula

Things do not change; we change.

—Henry David Thoreau

THE BIG IDEA
People buy when the product of their Current Dissatisfaction times their Future Promise exceeds the sum of their Costs plus their Fears.

There was a time when I would have told you that I absolutely loved my Boxster convertible. It was fun, sporty, and great on curves, and it provided me with a marvelous feeling when I drove around with the top down on a sunny day.

But it was also annoying in ways that increased over time. It was a soft-top, and the noise made it difficult to have a phone conversation. Replacing the tires required a second mortgage. I had to take the woods out of my golf bag to fit the bag in the trunk. When the car started to leak oil, I became very concerned about financial ruin.

Meanwhile, I longed to be back in a car that had a softer ride. I appreciated the Boxster's handling, but I missed the creature comforts of a luxury car.

Some peace and quiet in the cabin would also be nice. I am the world's worst parallel parker; a backup camera would be most welcome. Eventually, I began an online search and came across the Infiniti M series. I liked it!

Alas, there were drawbacks to purchasing a new car. There was the hassle factor in buying a car; I have never enjoyed that experience. And the Boxster was paid for; did I really want to shell out the cash for a new ride? And how did I know if this was the best price? And how would I get rid of my current car?

All the elements we have been discussing are present in this scenario. I was considering a purchase because I had grown uncomfortable, but competing discomforts sought to keep me from making a change. The familiar was no longer desirable, but it was . . . well . . . comfortable.

Think back to your most recent car purchase. As you evaluate that purchase decision, you will find direct examples of all the elements we have discussed thus far:

- **Current Dissatisfaction.** There had to have been something wrong with your previous car or the circumstances surrounding it; if there hadn't been, you would have had no desire to purchase anything else.

- **Future Promise.** There had to have been something appealing about your new car, something that drew you to the vehicle.

- **Cost.** You needed to deal with the expense, the payments, the hassle of purchasing, and other financial considerations (maintenance, insurance, and so on).

- **Fear.** You had to ask yourself whether this was the right car, the right time, and the right price. We are often constricted by our fear of making a poor decision.

THE BUYING FORMULA

Every purchase decision we make passes through a process of weighing the pros and cons, although we do this largely on a subconscious level. I have developed this process into a formula that I have taught to thousands of sales professionals.

People purchase when:

Current Dissatisfaction × Future Promise > Cost + Fear*

Think about the buying factors for any prospect you've ever worked with, and then place the influencing factors for each element of the formula on a rating scale. You can also think back to the last car you purchased; if you do, you will see the weighting process that went into that decision. Invariably, you will find a combination of all these factors.

So if you owned a car that was getting old and requiring more maintenance (high CD), you fell in love with a new car during a test drive (high FP), the payments seemed reasonable to you, and you trusted the dealer (low C/F), you moved forward with the purchase. If you came close but did not pull the trigger, it means that one or more of the variables were out of line.

THE FORMULA PROGRESSION

My wife and I were in Venice, Italy, a couple of Novembers ago. We noticed something almost immediately: it was cold! Not sweater cold, but heavy jacket cold. Venice was our first stop on a 16-day trip, so something had to be done. Because we were going to be in Europe for the next couple of weeks, we wanted to stay away from jackets that screamed, "I'm a foreigner!" We each purchased a black wool trench coat (and black leather gloves, of course). It didn't hurt that everything was on sale, but we still spent more than we had budgeted.

---

*I was first inspired to create this formula based on a 1988 article by Harvard Business School professor Michael Beer. In addressing organizational change, Beer suggested the following: "Amount of Change = (Dissatisfaction × Model × Process) > Cost of Change." Beer credits David Gleicher with having created the formula (sometimes referred to as "Gleicher's Formula"). The late Kathie Dannemiller further refined the concept to "Dissatisfaction × Vision × First Steps > Resistance," applying the ideas to organizational change as others before her had done. I have taken the liberty to simplify the formula further still, and to apply it to personal change rather than organizational change.

Did you notice the progression there? It began with Current Dissatisfaction and was fulfilled in our Future Promise. The Cost and Fear, while higher than we would have liked, was low enough to allow for a purchase.

The formula I have laid out is progressive: the Current Dissatisfaction has to be in place before your Future Promise kicks in, and that happens before you begin to pay attention to Cost and Fear. After all, if my level of dissatisfaction is very low, I have no interest in your product. Whenever possible, you should be thinking through this progression using the same thinking pattern as your prospect. The customers' mission (the desire to improve their lives) begins with Current Dissatisfaction. Put another way, show me someone with a Level 0 CD and I'll show you a noncustomer. That person will never buy—why would she?

Now think of the typical product and sales presentation. How often does it lead off with, "We're having a sale," or, "Let me tell you why this product is so great"? That, my friends, is a surefire way to ensure that your product is defined as a price-driven commodity.

THE DANGER IN LEADING WITH FUTURE PROMISE

This discussion is not just about the all-too-common "Let's Make a Deal" price-first approach that typifies the Cost and Fear message. Far too many presentations lead with a massive feature-dumping description of the product. That approach basically says: "Open wide. I'm going to jam this down your throat, and then you can describe the taste." This might work from time to time if you already have a very driven customer, but we know that this is often not the case.

To illustrate, let me tell you that I believe I could make a killing selling women's jewelry. I know nothing about the product, but I know a great deal about the customer niche called "men." And because I know them well, I know that they are clueless in the jewelry store environment.

Consider the man who is shopping for jewelry for his wife, and doing so as a way of saying, "I'm sorry for that very stupid thing I did." (Trust me, I've been there!)

What questions would typically be asked?

- "What is she looking for?"
- "What would she like?"
- "What colors is she into?"
- "Gold or silver?"
- "Does she have pierced ears?"
- "What is her birthstone?"

"What is her birthstone?" You might as well ask me her precise cholesterol count, the name of her second-grade teacher, or the brand name of her mascara. The big problem here is that the typical guy doesn't know how to answer these questions. I'm not in your jewelry store because I know exactly what I'm moving toward; if I knew that, I'd have bought online and saved myself the hassle. The clerk is standing behind a counter asking me about my wife's birthstone, but I am only 94.3 percent sure that my wife has brown eyes. You really think I can describe what she wants in a necklace?

Remember what I said earlier: if you know your customer well enough, the sale will roll out in front of you—the customer will show you how to sell him your product. The salesperson would be much better off asking questions that would lead to a deeper understanding of who my wife is, and then provide me with an appropriate suggestion based on what she has learned.

For example:

- "Tell me about your wife—what is she like?"
- "Does she like to make a statement with her jewelry, or is her approach more understated?"
- "Tell me about your favorite restaurant, and tell me what she wears when she goes there."
- "Have you heard her mention something that is missing from her jewelry collection?"

- "What have you given her in the past that she really, really liked?"
- "Tell me about a favorite outfit that you like to see her in."

I would love to sell jewelry for a living, and I would specialize in selling to men who were shopping for their significant others . . . and were totally clueless. I would love it if someone trustworthy and fun-spirited asked me the questions I just listed. If she did so, she would learn everything she needed to know. Then she could really work her magic: "Based on what you've told me, I want to recommend this."

Whatever *this* is, there's a good chance that I'm going to say yes. And why? Because anyone who asks those questions is now the expert, the trusted advisor.

(And just to clear the air, my wife and I dance every time Van Morrison's "Brown Eyed Girl" comes on; I know her eye color!)

THE DANGER IN LEADING WITH COST AND FEAR

Do you ever just get in the mood to buy a nice item of clothing for yourself for no particular reason? It happens to me about every six years, most recently on a road trip. My hotel was across from a mall, and I wanted a nice black sweater. I'm not even sure why; it just came over me. I felt the need to do something for . . . me!

I walked into a Banana Republic to look at its wares and was greeted, verbatim, as follows:

> Welcome to Banana Republic. Everything with an orange tag is 40 percent off. Let me know if you have any questions.

This salutation might have excited some of you, but I was immediately deflated. I was not there for a sale; I was there to take care of myself. I wanted to appreciate the item of clothing so much that I didn't care about the price. In essence, I *wanted* to pay full price. The sales message actually diminished my enthusiasm, and I left without making a purchase.

Pay attention the next time you are in a mall or at a car dealership or in a furniture store. Notice how often the sales presentation begins with an attempt to lower the Cost and Fear. Salespeople have been conditioned to launch into the "deal of the day" discussion as soon as a customer walks through the door. As an observer of such things, I find it frightening to see how often this happens.

Think about this approach for a moment. The message to the customer comes across like this: "I can hit you up front with a price that is so low you will have to pay attention to my deal, even if you don't like or need the product." I'm sorry, but that is just not how people really enjoy buying.

VALUE PURITY

Consider shopping at Nordstrom; we all know that we will pay a bit more. I've heard my share of experts, trainers, and speakers explain that we are willing to pay a premium for truly great service, and I think that is part of the reason behind Nordstrom's success. But perhaps the real benefit that the store provides is the feeling that you are getting the right price. Not the lowest price, but the right price—the fair price, if you will.

> *Value Purity is established when the customer believes that the price is both fair and final.*

I call this Value Purity. This is the shirt, and this is the price—either it's worth it or it's not. There is no question as to whether I'm getting the best price. Value Purity is established when the customer believes that the price is both fair and final. The price is deemed to be fair if the customer can see the inherent value in the product. The price is deemed to be final if the customer is convinced that there are no better terms to be had.

When you lead with a price discussion, you force me to ask these questions:

- What's wrong with it?
- Why doesn't anyone else want it?

- How much lower will you go?

- Should I pay more for better quality than you have?

- How difficult will the negotiation be?

- Will I be able to walk away feeling that I got the best possible terms?

- Will this go on sale tomorrow?

If you truly desire to build your brand's strength, forcing your customers into this line of inner dialogue is not the best course of action.

Review those questions one more time and tell me what you see in terms of customer discomfort. We are literally raising our customers' discomfort level at the exact moment when we should be making it easy for them to purchase.

On the other hand, suppose that the CD and the FP were already in place, and that both factors were compelling the customer to move forward. Imagine that you had a coffee-worthy relationship with your customers, and that you understood their mission to a tee. Now you can utilize a compelling price discussion to your advantage:

So you've told me that you are really not happy with your existing sofa because it looks dated and has lost its support and comfort. And you really like this sofa—it matches your décor and it is very comfortable. Here's the best part: we have a special promotion starting this weekend that gives you an additional 10 percent off plus free delivery. Would you like to make it yours?

Don't miss the key message: if you start with the C/F, the task is nearly impossible. (In the example just given, the deal is really not that compelling.) But if you start with the CD and the FP, you will find that the work to be done through the C/F is minimal. Let's face it: if the CD is very high and the FP is very high, how much work do I have to do through the C/F? Very little.

APPLYING THE FORMULA

This would be a good time for you to set the book down and consider some applications. If you are in an environment with a long sales cycle (where you track leads over a period of time), go back and evaluate the formula as it applies to several prospects you've been working with recently. If you are in more of a one-visit sales environment, think back on your most recent presentations.

It doesn't matter whether the customers purchased or not; we're just looking for real-world examples.

Take a good look at those recent customers and ask yourself these questions:

- Do I really understand their mission? What is it about their life that needs improving?
- What is their primary CD? Can I describe how it affects them on an emotional level?
- What is their primary FP? Can I put that in emotional terms?
- What are the major C/F issues? How early in the sales presentation did I talk about Cost? Could I have deferred that conversation until the CD and the FP were in place?

If you get this right, you can dramatically affect the buying cycle. When you spend more time on the CD and the FP, you'll spend significantly less time on the C/F. Talk this concept over with a manager or peer. It should not be difficult to find the application of the formula to your everyday sales experiences.

USING THE FORMULA TO REDUCE DISCOMFORT

Before we end this discussion, I would like to revisit the way the formula interacts with the customer's discomfort. On the surface, it would seem that the sales professional's task is to lower that level of discomfort. I don't happen to believe that.

On the contrary, I would contend that our objective is to increase the customers' discomfort with *the idea of doing nothing.* I have said all along that the reason people buy is to improve their lives. There is an extension of that principle: the sooner they move, the sooner their lives improve.

The sooner customers move, the sooner their lives improve.

Your customer needs to realize the discomfort resulting from *not* buying your product, and I believe the formula makes that clear. The formula highlights and then elevates the CD, then solves it with the FP. Lowering the C/F is just an enabling action, the logical price to pay for an improved life.

This is the beauty and the magic. It's not about how great the deal is, and it is certainly not about my slick presentation. The sale is based upon a raging CD, a striking FP, and a manageable level of C/F.

Some of you might be thinking, "Hold on there, big guy; the terms of the deal are what my customers want to talk about." I understand that, and I'll go even further. If I'm buying a car, that is precisely what I will lead off with . . . unless the salesperson takes the conversation in a different direction.

The truth is that deep down, I don't really want to buy something just because it's a great deal. Don't get me wrong: I love a smoking deal as much as the next guy, but *there is no such thing as a great deal on something I don't like very much.* Moreover, there is no great deal if the purchase does not improve my life.

To illustrate, I can get you a fantastic deal on a home right this moment. You can have it for $6,000—that's right, $6,000 and it's yours. That is not the down payment; it is the final price. That's just a little more than $30 a month. This is not a joke—I can get you that deal today . . . on a fixer-upper in a "not-so-nice" area of Detroit. Is it a great deal? Not unless it improves your life somehow. Let's be clear; it's a phenomenal price, but it's not a great deal. Make sense?

ALLEVIATING DISCOMFORT

The thing that lies at the foundation of positive change,
the way I see it, is service to a fellow human being.

—Lee Iacocca

My physician's job is very complex, but his mission is actually quite simple: he exists to decrease his patients' discomfort. Whether that discomfort takes the form of physical pain or the form of fear (a cancer scare, for example), he is at his best when his patients leave his office with a sense of relief.

This is your calling as well, my friends. I have dedicated much of this book to dealing with your own sales discomfort, but there is a greater payoff out there. When you are operating at your very best, you serve your customers by lowering their discomfort in moving forward with a purchase decision. In a sense, this entire book has been about your customer, not about you.

All that is for naught, of course, if you are not willing to apply what you have learned. But if you have been looking for that extra edge in your own performance, here it is. Dismantle your addiction to comfort, and you will change someone's world.

Questions to Ponder

- How does the Buying Formula help explain the conflicting thoughts that customers struggle with as they work through the decision process? What benefit does this understanding provide you as a sales professional?

- What will happen to your ability to win the sale if you do not understand each of the elements within a customer's Buying Formula? Reflecting on your own sales presentations, do you have a tendency to focus on one particular variable in the Buying Formula at the expense of others? How can you adapt your approach to cover all the variables?

- How well do you truly know your customers? Do you know them well enough to allow them to roll out the sale in front of you? What bold changes can you make to begin knowing your customers on a deeper level?

- How can your own boldness enable you to improve other people's lives?

Now Try This . . .

Think of the customer whose Current Dissatisfaction, Future Promise, and Cost/Fear you've been tracking over the past few chapters. Now, put everything you've learned so far into the context of the Buying Formula:

$$\text{Current Dissatisfaction} \times \text{Future Promise} > \text{Cost} + \text{Fear}$$

As a final step, take everything you know about your customer and answer these final questions:

- How can you amplify his or her Current Dissatisfaction?

- How can you amplify his or her Future Promise?

- How can you lower his or her Costs and Fears?

- How can you help this customer change his or her world?

Pro Customer Interview: June Steckler

June Steckler, my freelance editor, is a bit of a clothes/shoes/stuff horse. She likes to say that if it weren't for the obvious factors of reasonableness and closet space, there might be no end to her shopping. June casts a wide net when it comes to shopping and can be found both in high-end boutiques and at Grocery Outlet, the latter of which she readily admits is a word combo that gives one pause. In addition to doing her own retail shopping, June is a personal shopper for a few women, and she and her husband have bought, remodeled, and sold a couple of homes. This combination of facts made June the perfect "pro" customer for me to interview.

As you read Part III, what stood out to you with regard to the ideas of life improvement, Current Dissatisfaction, and buyer urgency, from the perspective of a customer?

What stood out to me first was the sheer truth of the improvement and dissatisfaction ideas. While I am one who loves shopping and may wander into a store simply because I am drawn in by a beautiful window display, the truth is that something about the appeal of that visual triggers these responses—desire for life improvement and dissatisfaction—on a subconscious level.

Can you recall specific experiences when you have encountered to and from salespeople?

I can, although I must say, to salespeople are far more common than from salespeople. When I read this section, I realized that I (again, somewhat subconsciously) sometimes try to circumvent the to approach by providing my from facts right off the bat. I hadn't fully thought this through until I read your book. As a time- and stress-saving device, I've developed this strategy to avoid receiving information (all the to facts—what you call feature dumping) that I know will distract me from my goal. Because I am, ahem, what you call a "pro customer," I am less stressed by shopping than most people. So, my discomfort lies more in the experience of salespeople who are pit-bull-level committed to their pitch versus really hearing me. I can't stand this, actually. And, I find it particularly off-putting when I do start with my from facts and they still adhere to whatever sales agenda they have in mind. I can understand having a to sales agenda, but when I cheerfully serve up the realities of my reasons for shopping, and salespeople respond with feature dumping or tell me about how something is marked down, I think, "They just don't get it," and I try to get away from them as fast as possible. I have and will pay more for something if it means I get to work with a salesperson who "gets me." As you say in your book, price isn't the ultimate motivator—it's about interacting and relationships.

OK, given all that, what is the very worst thing about to selling for you?

The stress that it adds to the buying experience. Like every customer, I have my reasons for buying. When a to salesperson is drowning me in information that I don't necessarily want or need, I have to keep reminding myself of what I want and why I'm there. Having to do this mental work of reminding myself over and over is stressful. It's like trying to talk to your husband on the phone when your kids are talking to you in person. It's too many voices at the same time. I'm sure no salesperson wants his or her voice to be the one that a customer is trying to tune out during the buying process!

Is there anything in this part that really resonated with you with regard to your work as a personal shopper?

Yes! The part about personal urgency and circumstantial urgency is what being a personal shopper is all about. Your advice to salespeople to go deeper, even if it's uncomfortable, in questioning and therefore knowing their customers is crucial. As a personal shopper, I find myself in the weird position of being both a salesperson of sorts and a customer at the same time. Because of this, I've developed a questionnaire that I have my clients fill out before we start the shopping process. Obviously, most salespeople do not have the benefit of being able to do this, but the questions and concepts in my questionnaire are exactly the same as what you present in this book. Frankly, a person's approach to buying is all about his or her past experiences. Personality really has less to do with it than one would think. So, again, being a from salesperson and taking the lead in asking the questions that allow you to know your customer more are the keys to success.

Afterword

Throughout this book, I hope I have provided you with countless opportunities for contemplation, decisions, and action steps. Now it is time for you to do something with all that. The best ideas in the world are useless without implementation.

From time to time, I have the privilege of hearing from sales professionals who tell me how my presentations and instruction have had a profound effect on their careers, and even on their lives. I truly appreciate hearing this. But I also realize that the real praise has to be reflected right back on those very same salespeople. My message goes out to thousands of sales professionals every year. The ultimate success does not come from the message; it comes from the application.

So it is with this book. I hope I have left you at a point where you are educated, inspired, challenged, and appreciative of the time you spent reading it. But it will all be for naught if you decide to put this book on a shelf without taking action.

Let me leave you with some final guidance on what to do next.

ON YOUR MARK . . .

First Step: Refresh

I hope you have read this book actively, with a highlighter in your hand and perhaps a journal in which to record your thoughts along the way. Now it is time for you to go back and review those sections that really stood out. Here are four focus points to keep in mind as you do that:

1. Review what you have learned. Pore through your notes and recall the most important messages throughout the book.

2. Hold on to the aha moments. Stop and meditate on those areas that really caused you to pause in your tracks as you were reading. Recall how you felt when you had those significant moments. Feel the energy and the emotion.

3. Embrace key discomforts. By now you know that the goal is not to avoid discomfort, but rather to embrace it. Feel the joy and the victory in being comfortable with your discomfort, knowing that discomfort means growth, and growth means success.

4. Study the principles. Go back and look at the steps to find out how you can use your discomfort as a launchpad. Read your notes and consider how you will apply what you have learned.

GET SET . . .

Second Step: Commit

In between knowledge and action is commitment, a stirring need to make a pact with yourself that you will take what you have learned and leverage it into long-term success. The stronger the commitment, the more likely the success. Don't take this lightly. Write out your commitment in very specific terms, and then find an accountability partner to help you. Here are some ways in which you can break down your commitment into a realistic plan:

1. Decide on what you want to do. Make sure you have a very clear action plan for how to attack that monster discomfort. The same goes for the smaller day-to-day nagging discomforts. Every discomfort requires a plan of attack. Reread your notes and create some kind of cheat sheet for yourself—visual reminders of your plan. Then write out your firm decision in very positive and encouraging terms.

2. Pledge to move forward right away. Don't just decide to do something; do it *today*! Give yourself very clear goals (daily, weekly, monthly, and so on) for what you want to accomplish. Remember that establishing a new habit takes 21 days, but they must be consecutive days. Keep that in mind as a guideline for getting started.

3. Discuss your commitment with someone else. Seek accountability through a friend, a manager, or a colleague who will push you to stay with your decision. Give him or her very specific instructions for how to keep you accountable.

4. Join the conversation. Visit www.beboldcommunity.com and share your insights, challenges, and commitments. Talk with others who are on the same journey. Encourage, and be encouraged.

GO!

Of course, refreshing and deciding are just the precursor steps. The real power comes through action. It would be a shame to have come this far and then not take the action steps. Ideas make us interesting and decisions make us motivated, but it is action that makes us effective.

I warn you that there will be a voice in your head telling you that knowing the material is good enough. That's a story, my friend, a rationalization for inaction. But that is *not you.* You are a bold, discomfort-loving, action-taking selling machine!

Take action, and take it today.

Thank you. Thank you for joining me on this journey. Thank you for investing your precious time in learning how to dismantle your addiction to comfort. Thank you for all you do for this wonderful industry we call sales.

At the end of the day, your customers are inspired by the same goal: the desire to improve their lives. That, my friends, is our high calling. We are privileged to help our customers to a better way of living.

Now go out and change someone's world!

INDEX

Heading: page numbers with an n indicate note.

A

Action:
    vs. attitude, boldness, 97, 103–104
    commit to plan for, 250
    decision → discomfort → action in CBT, 127
Adams, Jim, 191–192
Adams, John (Colonial era), 38–39
Advance preparation:
    decide on response, 145, 146–148, 151
    for major discomforts, 169–170, 175
    making decisions, 111–114, 130–131
    for minor discomfort, 144, 146, 151
    story creating and practice, 145, 148–150, 151
Aha moments, valuing, 250
Allen Edmonds shoes, 81
Ancowitz, Nancy, 72–74
Anticipate major discomfort, 172–173, 175
Anticipate minor discomfort, 144, 145, 146, 151
Apparel sales, 80–81
Aristotle, 19
Ash, Mary Kay, 54
Ask for the sale, 62–63, 82
Ask probing questions (*See* Questions, ask probing)
Assessment, SPQ*GOLD® for Sales Call Reluctance, 9, 13
Attitude:
    vs. action, boldness, 97–98, 103–104
    surprise discomfort, 158, 160
Automatic thoughts, 59–60, 143
Automobile sales, 122–124, 192–193, 235–236
Autoresponses (*See* Surprise discomforts, autoresponses to)
Awareness of story, gut check, 83–86, 185

B

Baldwin, Alec, 168
Banana Republic, 240
Barker, Larry, 19–21
Beer, Michael, 237n
Behavior (*See* Cognitive behavioral therapy [CBT])
Behavioral Sciences Research Press, 9
Big Idea:
    boldness as action, 97–99
    boldness begins with discomfort, 5–8
    boldness/comfort paradox, 179
    build boldness with advance preparation, 111–114
    buying formula, 235
    common discomforts, 139–140
    dissatisfaction and urgency, 197–198
    do the uncomfortable as soon as you sense discomfort, 157–158
    FP as solution to current dissatisfaction, 213
    gut check, 75–78
    major discomforts, 165–166
    master automatic reactions through repetition, 165–166
    Moment of Discomfort → Moment of Decision, 37–38
    overcome cost/fear, 225
    practice to retrain your brain, 125–126
    rationalization as success killers, 55–56
    small victories lead to big wins, 139–140
    surprise discomforts, autoresponses to, 157–158
    you are your actions, 19–21
    your standards are what you accept, 75–78
Blink (Gladwell), 59
Bold, defined, xix

253

ABOUT THE AUTHOR

Jeff Shore is a highly sought-after sales expert, author, speaker, and executive coach. For nearly three decades, Jeff and his team at Shore Consulting have guided executives and sales teams in large and small companies across the globe to embrace their discomforts and deliver **bold** sales results.

In a crowded field of sales experts and training programs, Jeff Shore stands out with his BE BOLD methodology. Combining his extensive frontline sales experience with the latest cognitive behavioral therapy research, Jeff has created a highly effective, personalized way to reset sales paradigms and deliver industry-leading results. An in-demand speaker, Jeff is able to demonstrate the power of **boldness** and connect with audiences using personal stories, real-world sales examples, and his trademark humor. Jeff doesn't just teach you how to sell; he shows you how to change your mindset and change your world.

Jeff Shore is an acclaimed member of the National Speaker's Association and a member of the exclusive Million Dollar Roundtable. He is a frequent contributor to leading business publications and the author of five books on a variety of sales-related topics.

Jeff and Karen Shore–married nearly 30 years–live in Auburn, California.

CPSIA information can be obtained
at www.ICGtesting.com
Printed in the USA
FFHW011450091219
56848702-62493FF